Liberated Publishing

Presents…

LiberatedPublishing.com

Liberated Publishing Inc.
1860 Wilma Rudolph Blvd
Clarksville, TN 37040

Copyright © 2010 Lyrical Eyes.

All rights reserved. No part of this book may be reproduced in any form or by any means without the prior written consent of the Publisher, excepting brief quotes used in reviews.

The characters and events in this book are fictitious. Any similarities to real persons living or dead are coincidental and not intended by the author.

If you purchased this book without a cover, you should be aware that this book is stolen property. It was reported as "unsold and destroyed" to the Publisher and neither the Author nor the Publisher has received any payment for this "stripped book".

ISBN: 978-0-982552353

First Printing: March 2010

Printed in the United States of America

Throughout the storm that I have faced, Lyrical requires nothing but greatness. I am not made from broken bones and I am not drowning in a well that is so deep that I can not get out of. However; over my lifetime, I thought I was. It is one thing to know what you hold but it is another thing to hold it. I love hard because I don't want anyone loving me weak. I am not your ordinary because God made me extraordinary. I am a force to be dealt with. I am an instrument for him and he is using me everyday.

This is for you… Ashlee' and Camari

All you need is faith

~ Lyrical

All photos by Marvin Bell
Marvelous Photographs@gmail.com

Cover design by Kenlo Key
kenlokey@hotmail.com

Readers can visit Lyrical Eyes at
Lyrical.eyes@yahoo.com

The Definition of POETRY

"Poetry is the emotion of words that comes together to define a feeling of truth. It is the master of its own rhythm. There are no comparisons."

~Lyrical Eyes

"I've learned that people will forget what you said, people will forget what you did, but people will never forget how you made them feel."

~Maya Angelou

TABLE OF CONTENTS

This book is separated in 3 chapters, something easy and straight to the point. You will not find yourself reading something and then being clueless at the end. Not here.... I promise.

Chapter 1 pages 1-142   The storm

Chapter 2 pages 145-263   The forecast is changing

Chapter 3 pages 267-346   The sun is out finally

Your syllabus for this class

This book is to help you, not to hinder you. It is here to allow you too see that you are not the only person that goes through things in a relationship. You are simply not alone and your tears are felt. No one is perfect or better than you. No one can ever place judgment on your situation. No one can ever call you stupid for staying or selfish for leaving. We live in a world where pain is given so freely and trickery is handed out like bubble gum. But this book is to make you understand that there is a greater outlet than pain, it is called LOVE. It protects you, it nurture's you and holds you. Love is very still and reserved, it shakes you up sometimes, but it does not hurt you to the core of your existence. And honestly, I have been to that core.

My purpose for this book is too give you guided love. Love somewhat like a mother that will try to protect you from hurt. I have been through it, in hopes that you will not have to endure it or if you are having a situation that seems unbearable at least you know you can come to a place and meditate, get angry through reading and start praying, because it works. We are human and how God has made us, you will read that he gives us choices, he even gives us signs that sometimes we ignore to know that we should not have even went to that place but we did not listen. Then he even gives you things that you pray for to show you that you really did not need that, but you asked....so he granted.

This book is pain lived through, transition lived through and then finally peace I am now living with. I had to stop putting people and situations

before my own. I am a hard lover, so I care about everything but have realized that loving limitless is where love should be. So throughout this book, I am still learning. We are products of our environment; however we can always do better. I am an advocate of living better and doing what makes you happy for the rest of your life because nothing is promised. I live my life telling people everyday the simple words that I love them. However, those that have hurt me, I truly love them from a distance. We as individuals have to learn about grace and mercy... We must be modest and treat people as we want them to treat ourselves. We can not live in a world only caring about ourselves to protect one from getting hurt, but when you do better, you live better. When you have less in my opinion, you live more. Life is not as hard as we make it, we make it harder. God has to be in everything that we do. The relationship will not work without him in it.
PERIOD

In this book, there is profanity. That is one reason that I am a poet, because I am able to allocate certain feelings through words. At the end of the day, I do not care about judgment, though I have before. But as I started understanding that God knows my heart..... It became clear to leave it there. I had to make the ultimate decision, which many have, problems with doing. But when you make decisions with God behind it, which shows that you have the character of strength and courage. No matter how hard that decision is, it is a good decision.

So with this being said. Read with free intentions. Everything that you will read is what I have been through or someone in my life has been through, but

I made it to happiness. The key factor is that I chose to go through many things when as I got older I realized that I did not have too. As a woman we can not save everyone, though we try. Therefore as a man, you can not save every woman. We are equal; we came from the rib of a man, not the head. We are to be treated as queens and our bodies are to be treated as temples. Men are to be treated like kings and their minds not down played. We are in an era of raising our babies to know this because there is so much nonsense in the world, we are killing ourselves.

Prosperity, love and patience are what is needed to survive. I won't have it any other way and neither should you.

Chapter

Just Angers Me So.........

Lyrical:

Our love was that melancholy type of
performance that everyone in this
world would want
you complemented me in every desire
of my life
but you did not believe in us or that
time was on our side
nor did you consult with God before
you decided to say goodbye
I needed you to concentrate on what
was different...
feel the wind that was warm not crisp
be that everlasting feeling, that
wetness to our kiss

Cat:

I needed our love to bring you peace
be so solid you could hold it

when I was too far from reach
and you still feel me...but you lack
the sense of touch
and I the sense to know better
still trying to moves something
thinking I was saving us
when all along there'd been nothing
still I needed you
so this love of mine that I call ours
was merely a figment of my
imagination
proven by your exiting stage right

Lyrical:

see you were in love with the idea of
me
because real love would not have
removed
us ,or allowed us to budge
nothing would have been able to come
between
what reality and simplicity was
I felt you in ways that only my soul

could understand
you were more then a man
you were my friend at least
my mind was made to think
we could stand
but we fell
before the figment was even created
we were worth the adversity
damn why couldn't you just believe
in me

Cat:

or maybe it was I
that filled in the blanks
left by unanswered questions
with what I wanted to think you'd say
or vice versa
maybe you didn't see me
but thought you knew me too well
to ever have to
brilliant and beautiful
but flawed and out of focus
this wicked hocus pocus

that cast spells that looked like forever
only to get there and learn
it was just a dream
you don't love me

Lyrical:

You just think you do
you might even want to
because if you did
the harmony that we made
would still be here to exist
in every step I take
in every tear that falls
the feeling of love would still be free
and not abused by words
that you think would sooth me
because you knew you would leave
you created an open wound
when an accident never occurred
you beat my soul up
now I'm left with nothing
but a song that I am tired of hearing

Cat:

stuck on repeat
with all the batteries dead
in the remote to my life
and the button broken
from atop the radio of my
train of thought
I'd be rid of you too
of I could feel anything
but this longing for you
that angers me
every second that it lingers
like the scent of you
between my fingers
I want out too
but all along our problem was
I can't do things
like you do

Lyrical:

I cant just act like you don't mean
anything

I cant just act like you never existed
when everything that was in me
was of what we consisted
see we still made that radio play
even though the batteries were dead
we moved to the melodies
of the music that played when our skin
touched in our bed
I know I gotta move on and let this pain that now is
around go
but I love you and that is my problem
that just angers me so......

Collaboration with Ms. Catalina Byrd
from Baltimore, MD

Misunderstood

I heard the truth last night and in my heart I just died
I cannot express pain by shedding any more damn tears
To do that is to make visual that I still care
All that is done in secret, comes to the light
And you think I am misunderstood because I need to be done right
I cared enough to give you my soul; First mistake
And now what is left is a story that is about to unfold
I am full of sickening emotions, yes I must admit
My thought of us and what I wanted
Surly no longer exist

We as sisters and brothers we just settle
Do to taking and accepting risks

But let go of nonsense before you don't exist

All of your fault of course not, I just thought
You would remain true
But it is what it has become
You just doing you
No more running to the ice box
And looking in the mirror after a physical fight
No more holding my pillow for shelter at night
I realize that perfect is God and you are to be the image of him
And that you are not
I hold no grudges, I express no anger now you are what we were
When we first met
Nothing but passing strangers

The mental, physical and emotional abuse needs to cease.

Woman to Woman

Woman to woman can I please talk to you
I just need you to understand
All that I have been through
no disrespect but I loved that man first
woman to woman him leaving me for you.....hurts
I cried many nights, thinking he would come back
but whatever your doing, just please give me some respect
you have seen my child and that kills me inside
what you don't understand that my child is my pride
This man has hurt me and I hope he does not hurt you
I'm not naive nor am I a regular chick
I just have a family and what I am asking for is for you
to disappear quick

you see he stayed with me when this
man did not have shit
so as he progressed and moved through
his life
this man promised me things like the
ultimate
I would become his wife
possibly you might think I am stupid
for professing how I feel
I was caught in a situation, doing
what he often wanted
 woman to woman my heart is what
he flaunted
I gave him everything; I gave this man
my left lung
 I am just warning you, so you don't
begin to sip on this rum
woman to woman I wish you the best
with him
woman to woman I hope you never get
old
I can only pray for you and
understand life is what it is
 woman to woman soon you will be
writing this...

My Sister (starting an unhealthy relationship)

I sometimes worry about the decisions that we tend to make
 I wonder when things will get easier for our sake
Though I do not agree with all that you do
I know that this also pertains to me from you
 I care about our friendship that is why at times I remain silent
Not because I am scared of the outcome but to preserve a tear from ones eyelid
 You have been my sister through thick and then
And though you know what you want
 I feel different about what you need
What I mean by this is that in life things come and things go
 And your need for love is beginning to show

He anticipate what you need and what you want
His love will nourish you if you let him do his work
I believe if you be patient with yourself, God will place him at your door
Not someone that you have been lusting for
Realize that I love you and I love past the best friend title
Because we have known each other for more than enough time
You are my heart and I truly care about what comes your way
And what you are about to go through is something you choose to create
A person in not an investment, you can not make one what you want
They should already be packaged and your should be what they flaunt
I appreciate your zest to give someone your love
But pray about your situations and

Let God guide you and set your goals
Believe me when I say that I know
how it feels to hurt
But when at times you feel alone, you
can always call on me for support
I want the best for you and my
babies, and I know you do also
Regardless if you feel I am a lane and
we do not relate
As well as you do with others I am
still the one who have been the most
faithful and still remains the same.
But only through God am I alright
I can only tell you to think long and
hard about the relationship you are
about to start
This is not an easy road, I know this
first hand
It wears on your spirit and soul as
well as your heart
And even through I know you are a
strong woman, I will pray for your
strength and your decisions
From morning until dark

But what is the reason you are about to put yourself through
A change in every season
It is in me to be honest with you as you have done with me before
Whether I liked it or not I could not ignore
That you felt how you felt because you were included in my storm
I believe in giving encouragement and exploring a friendship that you longed to have
But do not short yourself and create a life that will have a lonely path
As you state to me we know what is best for us
And as I state to you we know what is best for us
I state to you as serious as I can rhyme some words on
A piece of paper
Believe and trust that I have your emotions and feelings in mind
And in spirit
And I am here now as I will be here later.......

Bring Him Back To Me......

When will you allow me to hold you?
And you stop thinking about him
When will you realize nothing works?
If I am not present in it
Have you not seen that I control all
things?
Even if you don't understand and
want to give up on me
Don't you know that I knew where
you were going to be?
Don't you see my child it is not him it
is me
I made things happen to see how
strong you really were
You were loosing your vision and I
created you and you are my super star
You started to believe in man and
began to settle for what was wrong
Especially when you compromised
your life and know that you did
Because your feelings were hurt and

your heart had you cry all night long
I placed someone else in your way
 And I know that you do not understand
But I had to allow you to see things in a different light
 I needed you to be closer to me and I needed to take back the steering wheel
You were going left, when you should have been going right
You were drifting from my hands
And I won't settle for that
 Your passion was too great
And you had the devil slithering his way in
So yes it is me and not him
And I know you did nothing wrong
I know you wanted to try
 But I had to turn him away and send him on
I sent my only son, do you think he understood
Why him, you all both called out to me

And then of course I came right on time
I have not forgotten you my sweet
I am just preparing you for another life
I realize you think you know
But how could you when I am the one who controls
All mornings and all nights
Many don't know when I am talking
Or even if I exist
But I know you know
Because if you did not, how could you begin to write this
I am your hands when the tears fall down your face
I am your eyes when you need visions because things seem to look so gray
I am that breath of fresh air, that cool breeze on the small of your back
I am that comforts when you cant take this world and some of its disrespect

Child I know you are hurt and want
things back how they use to be
But I can't give you that this time
When resentment has been set in your
heart
 Because if I did, this time you would
fall apart
I allow you to make choices but c
early you are suffering with ones that
you have made
And If I did not love you, I would
create a path that would lead you
astray

You are my creation; I designed you
just for me
I knew as you got older, things would
be so differently
Your angry and upset this time, don't
you think that I can see
 But I m not going to give you what
you want
I'm simply going to finally give you
what you need

It seems harsh and unfair, darling; I see your every move
 But I know what is best this time………for I created you

Running Your Mouth

You're talking to your niggas,
explaining how she was
You're depicting it in detail as if she
was a rug
You're explaining how you beat it up
And made her say your name
Your thinking you brought her tears
of joy
When really they were tears of pain
This woman might have been longing
for something
She might have been 25
But inside she always cried
She was lusting for your affection
She wanted to feel important
She thought by telling you that she
loved you
She would get your attention
But all she inherited was a name
What a low down dirty shame
In your mind she was just a piece of
ass

And in reality hearing about her in your conversation
The average would think she had no class
But wait, stop and imagine if this was your child, sister or friend
Be a man and begin to cherish women and get out the mentality of just getting some ass.

The Disappointment......
They Failed Us

Time and time again
we allow ourselves to try
to try to give a person our heart
to even just be considerate of
ones feelings and they fail us
We get disappointed because
we could never do a person
how they do us
we could never act as if a person
did not matter
were not even around or just
do things that were clearly just selfish
a person makes time for
who they want too
if a person wants to come around then
they will
if a person thinks about you then
they will call you
if a person needs you they will show
it

through honesty and not pride
no ego will be able to stop the flow of
something as simple as just the
avenue of caring.....
The disappointment comes from us
putting to much into someone that is
not
worth even a failure......think about it.

The Twisted Relationship

As I sit and heard the lyrics that you said
I felt that spiritually God had entered into your head
The emotions of the words that you spoke
Mesmerized my thoughts
Formulated my words that uttered I love you enough
Enough to know that you were here.
I had a boy trying to find himself
Find him in the reality of the world
That sliced his throat
But now over this phone behind those bars
2 many miles to walk, only 30 minutes to talk
A man was on the other end of my phone
DAMN
As I sat and reminisced about how

love was and how and what love is
I realized that mistakes were made
Games were played
Hearts were broken
Fears were faced
But as one now we embraced
We embraced the fact that with one body
You see 2 minds we only needed one vision
To live through each other eyes
You have the formula to my solutions
You see I have became you
And you have became me
And in our forever is our eternity
The type of eternity that needs no ring
We have a song that no one can sing
A musical piece that needs no producer
You became my drug and I became your user
I became lyrically inclined at such a young age
I prayed for a brotha to be able to up lift

Me and accept my gift of words and
finally today
And finally after 6 years my prayers
has been answered
Finally instead of talking about my
talent in a negative way
you figured you would connect and
have a place
So gullible I joined in the hype
You picked up a pen and graciously
and flawlessly you joined in
You let the words move you
Every vowel, every letter made a word
That soothed you and complimented
me
Your words suddenly became my
blood
The blood that we shed for each other
Through every fight, through every
agonizing
Sleepiness night
As you spoke I visioned the birth of
our son, vision the lessons well
learned

We have embarked on a new relationship
That has always been my fantasy
The thought that my man, not my friend
Can make love to me through words and not touch
This shows acknowledgment that we entered us………

The Hit, When My Eye Turned Black

I remember the day like yesterday
waking up in the morning
everything normal
like usual
but anger was rumbling
one soul was pacing
wanting to go to where comfort was
given
where my mom and dad
were
and nothing was awful
or insecure
but love was around
but not where I was on that day
afternoon turned to night
and there begun the fight
that compromised my life
I remember the hit
so vivid that when I sit back and

think about it now
it makes me livid
He hit me
my eye swelled
I screamed and in an instant
I became paralyzed with fear
but could do nothing but cry and
listen to this bitch
say " See what you made me too"
are you serious I thought
but I had to go into the bathroom
and start praying to God
I cried with all I had
as this man sat in another room
acting like he cared
as soon as he hit me
I thought about my daddy and
how I needed him at that moment
to come in an rescue me
but he was at home
and he could not hear me
but in my soul I was hoping that he
could feel me
My body felt like I was drugged with

so much cocaine
that I could not even describe the
pain
or how I looked
I just knew I felt miserable
my mold had been broken
I was bleeding internally
and it took more that a right hook
I will never be able to describe the
feeling that I felt
but no one deserves the physical abuse
when it is dealt...

Get out of it, because it will continue.
True Story

When There Is No Comfort

Lord you are my comfort place; you are my soul and my only friend
Please tell me why my pain has no end
I am torn, washed up and hurt
When does the murder of my mind begin to cease to some release
When is enough; enough so I can begin my life
When does the torture of love stop so I can open my eyes?
My laughs have turned into shallow coughs with an awful grunting sound
My conversation has turned into a whisper and now no one is around
The devil is busy I feel him like never before and breaking down my door
But I have you God
When things are just too hard for me to bare

I know that soon my lips will stop talking
And I will begin to stare
Happiness comes and goes for me
I'm starting not to care
I need it to stay around I guess
I need momentum and laughs
To break deaths greary sound
I often wonder why I have to be a witness to so many things
But then how can I question you
The creator of all who believes
See I know you give us choices
And this is the choice that I chose
If I could go back a couple of years
I swear I wouldn't have even spoke
I surrender father
My heart, my conviction and my mind
Please from this day forth for the rest of my days
Let people be gentle and kind
I have rebuked satin in so many ways
But I am seeing him more and more each day

With my hands lifted, one up an then one down
I am in pain because one of the devils demons has hit me another time
But Devil you can take your knife back
God's pulling me from this fire............

Your Immaturity

Your immaturity shows
your loss
no gain
my stress let go
no pain
seen games
a mile away
your base
a distant restraint
your arrogance
no shame
however real love
for you will be displayed
I should have listened
and it would not be this way
I would not know you
and you definitely would not know me
the game you spit
would have been seen of that of bull shit
being mindful

of how you treat one
is always a good trait
because by doing one wrong
knowing that you are going to c come
back
but now the conversation is going to be to
kiss my ass.....

Cheating

The definition of cheating is the
direct contact of lying, deception,
fraud, trickery, imposture, or
imposition.

Ask yourself are you one of these or
have you ever been
The answer is for me yes
I have been that and done that
so that life style is not being lived by
me again
it is imperfection at its peak
and it hurts whoever your are with
once they seek
and whatever is done in the dark
will come to light
so trying not to buy that light bulb
its not needed
the sun stays bright
Cheating is trickery at its finest
it is the conversation of revelations
it ends before it ever really begins

it is Satan winning what he wants
it is being played while he continues to taunt
it is misery that follows a life of mystery
it is what has been seen or often tried
it is having your cake and eating it too
though I hate that phrase
one knows that is what we do
it is pain that often has no gain
it is reality that can make you insane
it is dominance at the top of its game
it is inconsistency with no refinery
it is infidelity that can cause no residency
it is a song with lyrics
that causes insecurity
that really started from no security..........
Cheating leads you back to you

12 Years Young

As I sit and look at the pail blue sky
Nothing but water flow across my eyes
Different thoughts start to enter in to my brain
As my heart starts to leak blood that will leave a permanent stain
As a woman you want a quote on quote man
Someone with a tough physique but whom will understand
You want their love to be tender and a life to be sweet
You want their hands to be tough and their center to be meek
I saw a 12 year old today

Not knowing how precious life is
Not knowing experience will teach her
And to think she has not even had her first kiss
As I scoped her personality from what life has to gain
I prayed for her in an instant
To be strong in the game
Game meaning life, prosperity and poise
Something she will witness when she is finished with her toys
I wanted to have a conversation just to sit her down to explain
That when you are young, you will go through some joys and pains
I wanted to take her my the hand and tell her never to fall

in love
But then I thought to myself she
is still pure as a dove
She knew nothing about love
Probably only from her mom
and dad
Maybe it is only me
And just my experiences and
choices have got me mad
I wish I was this child
With only adolescence to go
through
But unfortunately I have passed
that up
And my child hood years are
through
My midnights are even darker
And the 12 years old skies are
lighter
Her heart is empty and yet still
free

Mine is decrepit and empty
That is why it bothers me so
Because I happened to be her
only 12 years ago
I am 24 now and listen to how I
feel
I am a victim of love gone bad
I am a victim of a man
My midnight blues anyone can
steal

The Drunk Night

You came into my life
One night when I had been drinkin
The breeze was cool, the night was young
But inside my hear was sinking
To my surprise you pulled up
Not knowing what was about to happen
I fixed it in my mind to continue to groove with my girls
Ignore you like the others
But I was fronting because I wanted you
A conversation between the cars began
Laughter begins to arise
But something catches my eyes
5 women, 4 men converse
All looking like we were rehearsing for a play
Again I had been drinking on this day
I saw a smile that was warm and nice

I saw a life to continue with mine
I saw a man that I knew I could love
But my heart saw a nigga, like the one I had at home
In a matter of minutes my mind and smile shifted
My flirtation turned into desertion
My conversation with this man turned cold
I told him what he could not do
Not knowing what this man could offer me
Not knowing that if he gave love it could be true
No one knew in my circle of friends
What my hear felt at that time
But inside my body was yearning for this nigga to enter my mind
I knew if we both pulled off
With no type of info exchanged
The life that I had at home
Would continue for much to long
Suddenly he asked for my number
And I replied sweetheart you are to young

Stupid of me to say that, just trying to protect
Him from getting involved
But wanting him like the words to a song
So instead he gave me his
And I acted like I didn't want it
Not knowing the next morning
I was actually going to call him
Fuck what I was going through
I needed someone new
Those 5 minutes had changed my life
I needed some one to massage my insides
I needed someone to be serious with my mind
And 2 years later he is still around
I thought to my self if I would have never turned around
Through that window, there would have not been a sound
My life would have just been confined
And would not have consisted of you
Love has many faces
Pain, walks a straight and narrow

line
If you never attempt to start over
You won't be guaranteed another time
You will know when it has approached you
So do your best to not let it go
If you happen to let him slip by
You will find yourself alone

Married Men

Dude you are married
Would you quit sweatin me
All up in my ear, on my texts
Pestering thee
What the hell you get married for

You didn't check all the warning
signs
before you entered the door
you weren't thinking about me
When you said I do
Now were you?

Nope instead it was about the pretty
dress
How crisp that lining was
How all ya guys came to support
Yep it was about that ring, that
woman now sports

Please stop calln me talkn about you
made the wrong choice

No you didn't partner
Cuz I am not going to be the reason for your divorce

Hell to the naw, I'm not going to hell with you
Cuz in my bible it says
Adultery affects the next
And honey please the next wont be me

Uggghhhh here you go again
Same old lines
"She is just pissn me off with all this wine'n"
Well how the hell you think I feel
Calln me trying to make me feel like
You got what I need
Negro please
I was not a thought in that distant memory of yours
It is not my fault that my door is not open

and your have to go back to yours

Listen go home and pray
Get that wife of yours and take her
out on a date
Treat her like you did the first time
you saw her face
Wait a minute stop telln me you can
only see my face

Let me give you a word of advice
Now listen to this slow
Bet you, you see her face if she sees
mine
Now that's fo' sho
Listen I got to go
Some one is on the other line
Damn here goes another piece of shit
Let me now listen to his sorry ass
behind...... Deuces

My Verbal Mister

God send me someone that is going to
love me for me
who is not going to put his hand s on
me because of his insecurities
You see lord I keep going back
I am a child of unwarranted decisions
but I have learned patience so I am
praying for this mans deliverance
see God he has hit me so many times
that he has put me in places that I
hated in my life
he caused blood to show up in places
it should not.
an then I would look at him and feel
bad for him after he laid
his hands on me and I should want
his soul to rot
U gave me this talent of words
something that I do not have to
rehears
something that allows me to be free
something that can't be taken away
from me

even though he claims he has tried
he has even taken my poetry
and talked about it
which angered me so
and made me want question the
talent
you gave me in my life
but he is ignorant to what all I possess
he has no idea that he was messing
with God's best
I cry because he does not understand
what my
passion truly is
and because of his dominant behavior
I am letting this idiot win
See my mama was a poet
and she spit words when I was in the
womb
even when her life was hurting
and when she felt the most consumed
so I absorbed all the pain and was fed
through the umbilical cord
I was being prepared before I spoke
words
that were destined to be heard.

Eventually I know I will be doing
your work
but Lord I am tired; please send me
someone for me
because this fool tells me know one
will want
me
because of the burdens I continue to
heave
I need someone who won't strip me
from my words and make a mochary
of this poetry
I need a verbal mister who will not
live his life with constant "Baby I am
sorry"
I need him to acknowledge what I
have been through
and be able to say yes she went
through many things
but everything that she learned
sent her right here to my arms................
My verbal mister.

Have You Ever Sat In A Dark Room Just To Go Cry

Have you ever sat in a dark room just to go cry
Have you ever felt so alone that you just could not grasp why
Have you ever been around people and just thought to yourself if they only knew……
If they only knew
I have an epidemic in my life
I have been left several times
My mother gave me away; the men in my life all led me a stray
Have you ever listened to a song and the bass just vibrated through your soul
Have you ever listened to rain just tip toe on the ground?
I have always been self absorbed
When I get low I write so fast not slow

I work through my emotions but I
often get scared
I relieve the essence of my life
sometimes to be free
I am held captive within my self
I have never been able to be me
I so want to be set free. I want to be
someone else but me
I feel like a rattling chain that
analyzes my days and nights
I have visions of things that I know
are not right
I let my fingers release the evidence of
hurt when I write
I think about a different life
I am waiting for a deserved peace
A peace of life that will be fair
A sense of inquisitive moments that
cannot be shared
I am afraid of what is to come
I am myself to be strong
These words might not make since as
they are typed
But the physical inspirations of my
soul no one can ever write

The perception of me is totally wrong
Soothing music is in my head
Which makes me understand my restless nights
Which makes me understand that I will be emotional sometimes
Which makes me seek assistance from a higher power
The light that shines on my phasode
The rain that comes to help me with my pain
My sunshine is brighter than most because my demons I fight inside
I am caught in a world that forgives nothing
The balance is often not balanced
I am a victim because I am the abuser
I let myself go through things that I do not have to.
Release is so pure
Release is so pure
Letting go, tears will still come
Hurt know how to surface
How to show its face
That's what I am going through right

now
As I right and listen to Floetry
Minister to my soul and formulate my thoughts
Because things are always going to be
Because things are always going to be
And I am always going to be just me....

You Stood Still When The World Was Moving For Me………

Still hitting me and calling me names
Still spitting on my hopes and dreams
Still insecure when I am still here
Still wanting my goods, as you make me stay because of fear
How can you continue to hurt me and I know that you love me so much
But loving me so much, has turned you into a person that I can no longer touch
You have created a situation that has allowed me to see that the world
Continued to move, every time you call me names or strike me
And I have decided that when I saw midnight,
when the sun was out, something finally clicked

this union of ours was simply not right.
I am worth more than an a conversation of "you just made me mad"
I can not help you battle your demons sweetheart, inside your head
Time waits for no one and I believe this to be true
Because I stood still and let the world pass because of you
You may have beaten me physically and verbally once or twice
Maybe even three or four times
Damn I can't even remember, cuz this abuse has fucked up my mind
But all in all I am going to be okay
Because this nightmare made me stronger
To be a better examiner of a human today
You stood still, when the world was moving
And I allowed it to pass me by

But this time, I jumped for it
With all I had and left you with a smile
And not a tear in either eye..........

You and Me

I KNOW THAT YOU ARE GOING
THROUGH A LOT RIGHT NOW
AND I KNOW THAT THINGS SEEMED
FAR FETCHED BUT THINGS ARE
GOING TO WORK OUT SOMEHOW
I LOVE YOU MORE THAN YOU WILL
EVER KNOW
BUT AT TIMES YOU ARE THE ONE
THAT DOESN'T ALLOW YOUR
FEELING TO SHOW
WE CAN NOT SUCCEED IF WE ARE
NOT TOGETHER AS ONE
NOR CAN WE REACH OUR DREAMS
OR ACHIEVE OUR GOALS IF WE
CONTINUE ACTING LIKE WE ARE SO
YOUNG
I AM HERE FOR YOU BECAUSE I
LOVE YOU
AND I WANT THINGS TO WORK OUT
AND I WANT YOU TO KNOW THAT NO
MATTER THE STORM
OUR LOVE WILL STILL CONTINUE TO

STAND, STRONG NO DOUBT
I CARE FOR YOU LIKE YOU ARE MY KING
AND ALL I ASK IS TO BE TREATED LIKE OUR LOVING QUEEN
NOT ONCE A WEEK
OR WHEN THE MOOD SEEMS RIGHT
BECAUSE CHANGE DOES OCCUR
AND YOU STATED THAT YOU NEED ME IN YOUR LIFE
AS YOU ARE GOING THOUGH I AM GOING THROUGH ALSO
AND I NEED YOU NEAR
AND I FEEL THAT IF NOTHING IS ADDRESSED OUR FATAL END IS NEAR
WE JUST NEED TO TALK
AND BECOME THE BEST
AND NOT WORRY ABOUT BLAMING ONE AND EXCEPTING A STUPID FAULT
HELP ME AT THIS THING
BECAUSE I DO NOT KNOW WHAT ELSE TO DO
BUT ALL I KNOW IS THAT NOTHING

EVEN MATTERS BECAUSE OF THE
LOVE I HAVE FOR YOU

The Moment Of Truth

I wish someone would have came in and rescued me
When I thought I was not worth a thing
What I was doing which was actually staying, honestly was getting the best of me
I stayed in something that I knew I should have given up
But I thought that my feelings could solve it all
But this time it was not enough
See I invested so much time and part of my life
I love hard so my thinking that all the wrongs would eventually
Collide ...
But they didn't things just began to get worse
Secrets began to get created and respect just became a curse
Nothing mattered anymore but I stayed because

I don't know, just because I thought I
should
Thinking this situation would change
itself
Knowing in the back of my head, it
wouldn't
But then again it could
See I was never stupid
As some might tend to judge
I had became a person who was
simply in love
The situation was just complicated
So I ignored all the signs
Even though in my heart I was just
babysitting
What is called a lie
See when things are evidentially not
right
And you are trying hard to act like
the problems do not exist
You are hindering yourself
And your energy and mind begin to
take a twist
You start allowing yourself to deal
with anything

Even though you think you don't
But it is better to be alone
Because your heart will not steer your soul wrong
You have to listen even though your ears hear what they want
Because peace of mind is everything
And the moment of truth is what matters
And how fast we are moving is not.........

Games men play

Games men play are harsh and difficult. These games disturb the very part of you that makes up your inner piece. These games distort you, they hurt you, they confuse you, and if you are not strong enough, these games will break you and leave you speechless. We often find ourselves caught up in these particular types of games, based on the choices that we make. We choose to deal with men that are still in their boy hood phases. We choose to deal with men who refuse to be men. We choose to deal with men who are not worthy of us dealing with them, out of fear of loneliness. Because of pain we become insecure, timid and tired very quickly. We tend to believe them because we think they are sincere, when quite honestly they are not. We could think of a lot of reasons why men do what they do but instead of thinking of those reasons, let's be smarter ladies and choose not to deal with the games. The truth of the matter is, men only do what we let them, so let's stop letting them do whatever they are big and bad enough to do. Let's control how the game is played, by playing their game on our field with our rules, and our rules only.

"If he is intimated by your strength, he is simply not strong enough to deal with you"

Collaboration with my big sis..........
Rhonda Pickett, Chicago Illinois

What I am not (when a person questions who you are)

I was birthed from a womb that was prepared for me too soon
However I am not ahead of my time
I was raised in a wealthy environment
Contrary to ones belief I am not rich
But indeed I am valuable
My name means Dedicated to God
Honestly I am the first to state that I
Have violated that sometimes
I am not one to be stern or severe
Therefore I can speak with a gentle reprimand
My eyes are light with color
However I am not sensitive to the light
I am a sensible person
What I am not is heartless
So I am able to feel or perceive

Different circumstances in life
I have these talents of many
What I am not ….is quick to rush
To what I know is prepared and mine
Where I am going is to a location
With no designated time
What I am not is a person that is easy to push away
But what I am is a miracle in transit
I am blessed to be in my own space
What is impossible is attainable
What I am not is inconceivable
One will read up on me one day
What I am not is a southern mockingbird
However my vocals are from down south
I was raised in the northwest region
What I am not is septrional
I am passionate about my self being
What I am not is apologetic for how things come off
I am a very educated woman as many also are

My position in life is that of a strong
positive emotion
What I am not is complicated
However what I am is viable
What I am......is simply reliable
The definition of quantity and
quality love.....

Mastered Illusion

You said that you wanted a good
woman
in a whisper
and I appeared
you said you would treat her right
and I appeared
you said that you would be faithful
and I was there
you said that you would leave before
you hurt me
and you lied
you said that you were not cheating
and you were
you said that you would be honest at
all times
again you lied
see the situation about a relationship
that does not have God in it
is that it will never work
you can not hurt a person over and
over again
and expect them to still remain

the mastered illusion is that you will
live your life in vain
when will you ever learn that the
pressure will eventually cause you
reality that you are not ready to even
explain

EXOTIC AND EROTIC POETRY FOR GAMES PEOPLE PLAY

I want you to close your eyes
And imagine me and you together as one
One combined, see as hot as the sun
My carmel skin and your mahogany face
Sweat drippn as I squirt my love
Like a felon, believe me Ima leave a trace
Your dick between my legs. Yeah that's the right place
See I want you to yearn for me
Almost like you are about to get blue balls an shit
But that phrase don't mean nothing
Especially when our juices become equivalent
Equivalent to equal sex at its finest
See our chemistry

Is the essence of equality
That creates elasticity that makes
Me want you to mentally fuck me
Oh but w8 this is about me mentally fucking you
See me being a Scorpio means that I do what I say
Regardless of how it is seems
It is nothing for me to recipicate
And let alone you will never need to exaggerate
How I make you feel
When your dick enters my walls
And my exercises that I do begins to pulling you in
While you are pullin out
What you see on my face is nothing but a seductive grin
You looking amazed
While my clitoris
Is calling your name
And you are fucking me like you just got a multi million dollar deal
Not understanding that this shit I got

don't collapse, its stays wrapped
And yes this shit is real
See baby I am not scared of the in and
out and the trying anything new
Because of course there is something
that is in me that attracted us two
The way you pick me up and tell me
to wrap my hands around your neck
The way you position my legs to be
open while you are nibbling on my
clit
Ummmm yeah there are some things
that I want to do to you
See I can be your mistress and at the
same time be your boo
I also like mirrors, fuck one ,nigga we
need two
I need to see what you doin, and I
guess you can look in yours
You can ask me to do things that most
women would choose not to
See with me and you, there are no
limits to this passion fruit
Exotic, wet, sweet is me

With eyes that will make your sunrise
More complete
Got you walking around biting ya lip
Even got you clean up the house doing bitch shit
See I don't discriminate against much
Just as long as you come home and we begin to fuck....
Where I am, yeah you want to be there too
Cuz open up ya eyes, I was mentally fucking you....

Broken but not shattered

What's your name, he stated
with this raspy sexy voice
she stated I go by the name of
Beautiful
of course
As he looked her up and down
as she did him
the attraction became instant
The seduction took precedence
over both of them with tattoos
attached to their skin
like diamonds in their ears
She saw herself in him

The feelings of I want you now
Lingered in the air
pure gratification of being satisfied
was whispered in her ears

Some how he was turning her on
with his conversation
and she was turning him on with

her observation ...of him
Him that was making her think
futuristic bullshit
because his swagger was that mean
where ever he was she decided that is
where she wanted to be

As she tried to control her feelings
they were coming fast
And things were happening to her
shit that had never happened in her
past
She began to have fullness

He would talk about things that
mattered
Items that made her use her mind
Things she actually learned from
Intellectual conversation's that made
sense at that present time

Let me state that again
you see

He would talk about things that
mattered
Items that made her use her mind
Things she actually learned from
Intellectual conversation's that made
sense at that present time

somehow while the feelings were
brewing
he slowly entered into her world
she began to have those feelings of
hmmm maybe this boy likes this girl

as things progressed they became closer
at least that is what she thought
until she began to notice
that things were going wrong

see a woman's intuition is something
a man can never have
she began to have feelings of another
lurking
but she did not have the strength to
ask

see he told her things like I'll be
honest
all you have to do is question what
you want to know
but why would she bring up
insecurities as the 2 of them began to
grow

as her feelings became stronger his
began to subside
because he was starting to look into
her life
he did not understand that what was
in the past
was something sometimes to painful to
rehash
so instead of dealing with her he was
starting to question
why he was having feelings for this
student in his class

as time went on months had began to
pass
something was different

the time that once mattered
was not spent nor did it last
things began to change
curiosity haunted her
he was becoming distant
and his ears no longer listened

As she looked him up he was
registered as a
serial dater
So instead of being that of honest
He decided to hurt her later
He figured she was naïve because she
was inconsistent with her thoughts
However what he did not know was
that
She began to pray for clarity and
knew he would
eventually get caught....
see
He began to analyze and place
judgment on many
Different things
He decided he did not want to spend
time

As he knew she was becoming broken
inside
Her imagination took her to other
levels
To take away the arrogance and
confidence
that sometimes he often showed
his inconsistency with her
began to express his lack of concern
But change came with another
woman
So his heart and desire for her began
to fade
He let her feelings keep growing
Like running water that began to
wade

The heart and mind began to wrestle
with what
Her precious being was going through
as
She reminisced on her last intimate
time with him
Their silhouette of them in the mirror

combined the 2

What looked to be like 2 souls that were connecting
now she understands was deception
To her she thought maybe the sweat was his connection

she wanted his knowingness to be free
and try to allow them have some chemistry
but instead the course that he was teaching
she realized was history
He resisted what was new
All she wanted to do was nurture his reality
However he choose to do what some men do naturally

She began waiting in vain
Not realizing that her worth was more than restraint
That would eventually turn into that

of pain
you see if she would have thought
about
her instead of him so much
her heart would not have broken
because now a man to her
is a conversation to not be spoken

She was beginning to feel that she was
on a string
and began hearing whispers of let it
be
if he was meant for you
eventually you will see

Feelings are that consistent flutter of
the heart
That joyous feeling of anticipation
Of seeing what you can only hope
will be for you
Hoping that his love will be your
release
that stillness in your peace

However hers was not
She had a termination of a lease
See she was leased from God
And her heart was rented out
And if it was not for his grace
She would not be able to have peace
And still remain in a humble state

She hoped that he knew that she had
nothing but good intentions
But the more she knocked the less he
let her in
His interactions had finally changed
His status was that of another
Her not knowing what was going on
behind closed doors
She had trusted him with her
precious jewels
But she was blinded on what to do
Because now she loved this man
Especially when he would sing this
song
Concentrate on you.......

Though her heart was hurt, she was able to accept
That she put herself out there
And still to this day has no regrets
He was that of a gentleman to her
But it is believed his heart was scared
So other avenue's presented themselves
As she wished that he was still there
Because her love was sincere and at the end of the day
Her tears showed she cared.

And their story went to that, which became typical in a sense
A heartless conversation with tears on the other end
But to this day he will never know how they really were good friends
He had shades on to protect him from what was happening to him
Because the feelings and movement of his heart
She believed kept him on a limb

As she thought about their last dance
And how comfortable they once were
She can only reflect on him which is
whom she really adored

For The Men......

Trying to find something to get into
I am in complete solitude
Knowing that everything about you
Is what I think that I need
But understand that I got a girl at home
So this is not just about me
She is cool for the time being
But things at home are getting boring
She is nothing of what she use to be
I know that they say that the grass might not be greener on the other side
But from what I am looking like
Shit you look like paradise
The water looks clear
And I think I might need a glass
See this is about where your mind is
Simply not just about some ass
Don't get me wrong I love her
But love is not just what is suppose to keep a man at home
See we need understanding and help too

Not just hey honey, I'm going out with the girls all the time
Baby just go out with your guy and find something to get into
Now see every time she utters those words
I really did not think about what that meant
But I am tired of hanging with my guys
I need some quality time spent
See I see you looking at me like I am full of shit
But baby girl trust I'm a try, at least before I quit
You seem to keep my interest
And now I am stuck on what I should do
See when I go home, I am only going to think about you
See best believe if I was happy, yeah maybe this is not something
I would be going through
But right now, in my life

Home aint where the heart is
It seems to be staring at me from your eyes

Haven't seen you in a while......

He walked up to me and said "hey you"
And I looked so shy but I looked in his eyes
He said I haven't seen you in a while
I was thinking to myself.... Inside with a smile
That hasn't bothered me
Especially since you were one of the ones that caused me so much turmoil
You were doing you back then
Which has made me a monster with stilettos next to kin
He said "you look absolutely gorgeous"
I admit it made me blush
As he grabbed my hand
I felt the heat from his palm
Sooth my insecurities that I once had with him
But I remembered that even snakes were pretty

But they also slithered and knew how to shed skin
I told him "you looking like your regret the day we split"
He looked away and said I have never gotten over you
To my surprise I felt sorry at that moment
Because my tears were no more
And I was now more secure and it showed
First class love was what I had for him
And I knew he was standing there regretting all that had occurred
I wanted to tell him to now dust his insecurities of his shirt
But instead we conversated a little more
And I told him I had to run
Gave him a hug
And at that moment he held me tight
As if I were dead and came back to life

As I tried to pull away, he whispered I
will always love you and I miss you
And my body fell limp to his words
But my memory caught me and was
my spine
That was now in my weak back
As I heard what he said, I thought
wow
When I wanted to hear these things
You were cold and living in a vain
world that consisted of you
And now I hear you talking, but I am
good
Because I always knew the truth
Haven't seen you in a while was going
to be a statement
That was always going to haunt your
imagination and memories
And be your language of us two………

Tempestuous Pain

Destiny Equality

Have you ever wanted someone so bad
you couldn't see the light of day
when everything was clear as the
darkness went away
you had said something's that weren't
in your best interest
Contested with conviction what was
left of your existence
Resisted your ego and your revolting
pride
Were the stronger in the end to keep it
all inside
Although you didn't want to just yet
let go
There was something so uncertain you
didn't want to know

Lyrical Eyes

so we as humans carry along things with such pride
knowing that internally we are crying inside
not sure of what to do or what to say
only in your mind, words start coming
like have you ever......
wishing things in your past would totally go away
hurt, mistakes, pain and sorrow
knowing that even though there is a tomorrow
you are lost with out words
emotions and scars that haunt you
as you try to move on
try to cope with yesterdays issues
even though they are gone

Destiny Equality

They say the past is gone but it lingers in the dust

Where you can't seem to help fighting with resistance
In a selfish twist it becomes an obsession
And then I hear that song "I keep forgetting were not in love anymore"
The fear and rejection seems to overload with the tempestuous pain
Have you ever hoped that those that hurt you got a taste of happiness
The kind you have been neglected your entire life
Just so you didn't have to express your real feelings
Turning the other cheek wasn't always best
Almost like the blackness followed in every relationship
Whether we were best friends, sisters, brothers
Fuck buddies or soul-mates I hate to feel the hands of ambivalence
Pushing others back when it was clearly fate that brought us here

Lyrical Eyes

Brought us to the saying that
everything happens for a reason but
what is the reason that I am hurt
what is the reason why tears have
streamed down my face
and I still tried, tried so hard that I
felt as if I was in court
The court of the defendant being done
wrong
when all along I was there for you
all along I even sometime loved you
more than I loved my self
yeah I know that is wrong
but fuck it, nothing was being
rehearsed
everything was real
how I felt was the deal
the hand that I picked had you in it
and you were suppose to treasure it
not fuck it all up to put pleasure in
you
you that hurt me

when I was the one that always saw you through
I loved you when no one else did
I contemplated some many things with this shit
it was like even though you were hurting me
I was obsessed with the I'm sorries
when all along what you were giving was not love
you were just giving my soul and space worries......

Destiny Equality

Worries and quarries of passions so hidden proverbial and hidden
The love and compassion the resistance was convicted at trial
All along I waited patiently respected every protruding fear
Didn't have to keep it hidden I already knew
Have you ever tried to respect others

wishes when they weren't your own
How many times this has been said I have a mental block
We all have been hurt and we all have been lost love seems at a higher cost
As I toss the ashes from my cigarette and so desperately want to forget
The pain that steamed from those regrets you call it confusion
But the truth of the matter is it was an illusion
Since I was the maiden in waiting and he was the knight in shining armor
And the deja-vu was repeatedly calling
I am still falling so desperate to get my point across
Long since have given up on this notion
If were meant to be then so be it
But I still believe in love and can see it

maybe if we would have followed our
intuition the first time
pain would have never come
It is amazing to me how we choose the
roads we take
but at the end of the day our judge of
character was
really was the true mistake

Lyrical Eyes

As I listen to Tweet as I am smoking
my cigarette as well
I tip my hat to those that have been
hurt
let us not dwell on what was
but what is now
to learn from it and grow
to not desire the pain
because Karma is at the show
see when your heart is pure and
you have no choice but to move on to
the next

there are no reasons to have past regret
The resistance and rejection of broken
promises
and lies told
create pain and scars that become
shriveled and old
The price we pay for giving ourselves
to another
is a deadly cost at time
but you have to go through it because
the definition is that of
life
Confusion only comes when you do
not understand what has happened
but when you can step back and look
at your past
you place yourself in that optical
illusion of how you see your self now
When you place your self out in the
world
vulnerable is what we become
man or woman
how you feel about the other is sure to
come

but how you deal with it is another road
that you should have learned from
when you think back to what went wrong

Destiny Equality

We live and learn from those mistakes
heartbreaks as we take
I would hate to think it was all in vain
Blowing out like a candle in the rain
As the picture though your window
You might see right through my heart
For what is left without you without us
As I tend to think that it all can be resolved
Like good times and bad times
I think that it can overcome if we wanted to
Have you ever hoped that the universe wasn't a complete mysteries

And we could rewrite all our previous histories
Instead of insisting upon our wants and needs
Those things that we could quite conceive
I still believe as Brenda Kay did in the 80s
That maybe we are all on a breeze
And if we fail to seize the moment
We would be again at this point
Sparks fly and haunt reflections and ghosts taunt
But I won't continue to go through life this way
As I make it through yet another day

Lyrical Eyes

well spoken my sista
yes we live and we learn
and as life continues to guide us

pain in no longer excepted
my sign I wear says no longer will I mourn
We have overcome so much as humans
that I know personally things are not fair
but situations simply just make you have to care
What is conceived is a stronger person
even though it may not seem like it at the time
Happiness consists in the desires of our minds
Though we can not see the future
but only the streets that are ahead of us
refer to Psalms 140 and realize that
this is a prayer for Deliverance from evil men
Know that in life we are going to go through things
that we do not choose
But my dear soul know that in the storm
      God is using you.......

*Collaboration with Ms. Destiny
Equality from Miami, Florida*

Resisting Age..........

In a room where there are many people
There's a mahogany face with beautiful
Eyes like me
Eyes that control a destiny that he has never seen before
A situation that can move his life through opportunities door.
There is a heart that is young as mine use to be
A smile with a million words to say
A swagger that makes me question my position
In life today
As fine as he was
I'm surprised he noticed me
I hate that time is improvising on what should be
He is the epitome of what young love
Simply consist of

And if I were his age, I would
precipitate a conversation
That would penetrate every since of
the word
Relationship
Relationship meaning us
Us meaning a creation
Like a cool wet summer breeze
Listening to Jill Scott or De la Soul
Taken' trips
Layin' by some trees
In a fantasy world
I would march to his beat
Lay up and watch him press repeat
As he created music
I would create the same
I can imagine walkin' in to his studio
Placin' my hands on his braids
Mesmerizing his mind
And looking into his eyes
That were identical to mine
Reality became real
As he asked me how young I was
Words began to evolve

It was not by accident that we met
However he was my problem to solve
As I created numbers that were
Politely put into his phone
We decided to keep things a secret
And enjoy our time alone

A Letter From A 6 Year Old

I love you
I hate you
I do not understand you
I want you
To want me
Like I want you
Am I talking about a man?
Or am I talking about a child without him.....

Let me do this again
cuz these are my emotions

I love you
I hate you
I do not understand you
I want you
To want me
Like I want you

I am a child
That did not ask to be here
I am a valuable asset to not only
My mom's life
But yours as well
But see you don't even see that
But I know someday that you will
See you come and you go
But when I get older
That is going to be a hard situation to even deal
However you act like you are doing me a favor
By loving me some more
You somehow deep down inside do not realize
That me as your son is going to make it
Make it on another level
That you weren't even included......so please don't fake it

Like you, I deserve your time
Hell you made me

I deserve for you to see me cry
And not my mother all the time
But you come around when you need something
But I am so happy that my mommy did not let you back
With the same song that you always sing

See I am going to be a better man than you
Everything that you keep doing is the life that you choose
I got God in my life and pray to him every night
With out you,
See my mommy taught me how to pray
She taught me how when I don't understand
Pick up the phone and call her all day
Yeah I am only 6 but I am a king and
Definitely came from a queen

She is a poet and my mommy sings to me

See we talk and she has never made me an option
She tells me how not to be
And still does not even include your bad ways in the synopsis
She does not know that I know what is going on
So I play the role, cuz all she has to do is just hold on

You are only hurting yourself
To not grow up in my life
You keep doing things and you know they are not right
But my grandpa said he got me
So he sees me every night

I just feel sorry for you that it's not mommy this time
But it's me that don't want your mess

to hinder the many years
That are coming into my life

I am greatness
My mommy and sisters biggest success...

I Just Gotta Go

I sit and ponder on many many many
things
I even pray for interference so that my
mind can stop working as hard
I have been through things that some
think are a clutch for me
I even been through things that some
got the nerve to think is easy
and aint been through nothing that I
have ever endured or seen...
But let me say, when you do go
through your thing
I'll be there not to judge but hold you
up because unlike you I've been that
fighter in that same exact ring
See it is called being used
by the most precious high
He uses us to be that source of comfort
because I once had many sleepless
nights and could not understand that
ever so hard

question of why
but the difference will be I did not
ask it and I promise you will
because life is so easy and you take it
as it comes
how modest you are cuz I can't wish
such pain on anyone
My heart and mind move faster than
others
that I can admit
but best believe I will not fault myself
for how I live
not to really state a person is rushing
but when bullshit comes, I stand still
and then walk as I know I am about
to quit
it is not hard to do what you feel and
make things stable and legit
I like to get to what the core is
and work through the middle from
side to side
and see if I am even capable of this
shit

because everyone is not built for it
some commit their own death through
fucking up
and committing suicide
suicide with no intentions of even
understanding that
if you would have possibly just tried
that obstacle that you thought you
were facing
might have moved around and began
to surface on the inside
it would have formed a mold that
would have created that structure
of strength that could uphold
anything
but instead you decided to do what
was easy
and live what you think is reality
Sometimes I questioned things because
of how naive and dumb a person
thinks you are
when all along sometimes, you are the
one that is about to step out that
revolving door

It kills me when they think that they are better than most
let me tell you, it is a cold, cold world when your energy is not coming from the host
If only you would have just tried, but since you think you know everything here.......let me hand you your suicide cuz at this point..... I just gotta go

For Some Reason

For some reason you think you can
tell me anything
And it is suppose to be cool
For some reason, you think that
because I am with you
I don't have anything else to do
We have been doing this thing called
a relationship
For some years now
And I am tired of the back and forth
Tired of the not feeling appreciated
And when we fight, you got to go
make a run
Out the damn door
See I am tired of bickering like 2
howling dogs
That only get along when we fuck
And then the next day we at back at
it
Like we never touched
I am at my wits end with you

And you place the blame always on me
Naw it aint never you, so of course you gone agree
I am beginning to think that this relationship is just over rated
Nothing is genuine anymore
We act like strangers in these 4 walls
When we use to love each other from the skin to the core
You can't tell me anything
And just act like I am going to agree
You need to worry about the day that I stop speaking
What is really going on with me......?

In The Raw

While we made love last night
I reminisced about that hurtful fight
That consumed us both with wrongs
and rights
That almost took you out my life
I realized that things will come
And I realized that you might be the
one
As I feel what was familiar inside of
me
I understood the female anatomy
To urge for something that is not yours
To know at that time you were
involved in spirit
I spared you for someone else to feel it
I tend be optimistic as I do most times
But to insult my intelligence
Is where I draw the line
I will do my best to sustain my hurt
But no more hearing about you and
her

I can try to do the best as being your lady
But do not go off of what's been
Going on lately
I felt different knowing I was not the only one
But I have a sense of peace, your returned to me
Will I forget this part of us and move on?
I cannot promise you that but I can assure you
That the reason your mind shifted was because I am the one.

Moments of Love......

1.2.3. There is a moment that has already passed me by
4.5.6 How do I attempt to grab it and rekindle the fire
Of what do I hold dear to make my insides yearn with desire
Love of who can make me have a moment of my own sexual empire

Moments of this type of love is truly and experience
With where and whom, is an option that is actually yours
With being a woman, the every stroke of a ma makes you have to want more
The type of moment that I am conversation about if never short but very brief
Shit if you feel where I am coming from your precious pearl has many times already been released

Of what do you bite, when your insides are massaged so tenderly and right
Of what do you do, when you life is resting calm at night
But the urge of getting wet trembles in your ever so peaceful mind
Your thoughts begin to wonder and your body knows it's time

Love is something dangerous
It is a poison that affects the soul
It is a disease that is not curable
But an emotion that you can not control
It moves through out your heart
It dances in your spine
It even tends to play games
But definitely tricks that can confuse the mind
Although this disease it not lethal
The motions that it goes through are very different every time
It can make you feel warm and relaxed

But watch out now, it can also snap back
Injecting love into your blood stream can make you go through withdrawal
But that powerful machine that a man has can make you skin tremble, hell it can drive you up a wall
The power of it, my god a man that know about it, is nothing but blessed
He can be your stress reliever, so you can soon rest
Now if you look back up through this passage that has been written
You will see to your left side going down that moments of love is mentioned
There is a song that goes with these feelings
It is an instrumental
It rescues your deepest thoughts from your soul
The pounding of the beat makes you want to check into rehab for people that
Loose control

It gives you peace through
A since of well worth sleepless nights
Moments of love, something you
should have in your life...............

Little Thing Called Karma

See he said that my poems were really letters to another man
Little did this idiot know, he was disrespecting Gods plan
So I grinded harder and made my self come to light
And everything positive in my life
Was beginning to unfold and he became a thief in the night
See he told me, you got to much baggage and pain
Aint nobody gone want you
Little did this fool know that I was getting opportunities
That only celebrities do
See he told me that I was worth nothing and men were always going to want to hit
And I was not good for anything that's why I kept going through shit

Little did this ass know, I was signing a deal
While they were taking his finger prints
See he told me that I was crazy and I was a bitch for some things that I did
Little did he know that most of the things that were happening
Were because my feelings were what mattered and not his
See he told me you never sang for me or ever wrote something about me
Little did he know, I do not sing for evil and weren't you the same person
That disrespected my craft
Why would I also sing for someone that on the sly had beat my ass
See he told me I was dead to him
Even though I had this mans child
Funny how God works
Now God took him away from his child for a while

See for those that are always quick to belittle someone else

And not respect what is a talent or
love that one might have

In the end, it has always been done,
that karma will whoop that ass.....

I Got A Jones..........................

You disrespect my mental
To boost yourself to where you feel a flutter
You put the true definition in late night call
By using sex to define what you think moves me
How ridiculous you are to have never experienced what feeling good really is
How selfish it was for me to think that you could ever accept the anatomy of a real woman.
Your attraction lies in your skin, but defiantly not behind it
The thrill of uncertainty keeps you coming back
Because I show you nothing
I take the chemistry off the sheets we use and then you are gone
Until you call again

I ask my self, why I give in to this bullshit
Shit because it's good and because I need the trust and force of what lies within
As sweat drips countless times and my eyes role back in my head
I have to stop and think how many more women have been in this mans bed
No emotions shown because there is none, just seduction and conversation that gets me high.
This jones makes me exhausted
In a good way because I really don't give a shit
I'm getting what I need at this time
Although he thinks he getting me
In my domain I control my world around me
I answer every other time he calls
Yeah he leaves, me thinking
That why I allow him to call

The Break up

If I could get to you, I would tell you that I am sorry
If I could just give you a hug, I would tell you that I love you
If I could take back my actions, I admit I would have done them differently
But when you are under stress and unhappy, you do things relentlessly
I did not realize how much of am impact you had on my life
I say this because I ma reminded of you when I attempt something new
 I freeze up and become paralyzed
I replay some of our conversations so vividly in my mind
I remember how you loved my kids as your own, over years and time
 But I understand how people go their different ways
And I appreciate what life will teach

you if you happen to go a stray
Our depart has bothered me, when I
sit back and relive
And I know that I hurt you but that
was never my true intent
I did not know how to leave
And that is the simple truth
We had a relationship
And I was breaking up with you
Though that sounds like words from a
child that they would utter out their
mouth
But I pray as I sent you this for you
and your continued health
If I could change anything, it would
be that I know I broke your heart
Irregardless of what you say it was
more than business from the start
You were and are a powerful person
that I am proud to say that I know
It hurt me to be around you and not
be able to be real
Sometimes I did not even want to
speak to say hey or hello

To know that I can not pick up the phone
Bothers me
Don't get me wrong I am doing fine
But I go to prayer in spirit for you and me all the time
I simply just pray for closure
Because I miss you so much
And at times it affects me and I can do nothing but wipe tears from my eyes
And I pray for understanding on your end
And maybe a friendship because you were a friend from within
I have always been patient and have remained humble in my life
But you always taught me to be mindful of how you treat people
And I am sorry this one last time
But I had to go on my way
I will never forget you, we have too much together
I will unselfishly always love you

No matter how this situation unravels itself
But I wanted you to know that I learned from the experience
Please except this as an apology with nothing else allowed.

Me

See there was this cat that looked right when I saw him
He told me baby let me solve your problems
He said I am the person who will solve them
He said I was something out of a magazine
And my past hurt we would resolve them
He said he wanted to be part of my life so I allowed him
He said I would never hurt you
So naïve and ready to be in love
I believed him
He said this is the way you do things
So I followed him
He said this is how you speak
So he corrected me
An things that were important to me
He would listen and not ignore me

U see things that mattered to me
His ear was there for me
And his conversation
See it was there to sooth me
So as we got closer
His heart began showing insecurities
See all that in the beginning
wasn't moving me
He was showing signs of being selfish
So he eluded me
And at that moment
This concerned me
But because now I cared
This frustrated me
falling for a conversation
Instead of a man showing me
I was back on the path
Of being lonely
Which really started not to bother me
Because then I could not get hurt
By a catastrophe
Of a human making perfect promises
That he could not keep
And in the end

Me being beautiful
Brought me back home to go to sleep

Just a Rode

I am here
You are there
But some where we got lost to be
Where?
The answer is....
Where no one else could be
Where no one else would dare to go
Where no one else could see
Simply that loves for you an me
You are there alone as a man
Trying to depict what happened to
your life
Wondering is growing up
As hard as cutting a watermelon with
butter knife
See I am here content with where I am
Understanding that possibly later
Here is where I would stand
Stand confident not alone

But still not holding anyone's hand
Together we personified lust and like
At the same time
We created distance that somehow
drew a line
A road that would allow us somehow
to meet up again
But is again now, or was it simply
then
See did we meet each other at the
right time
Even though things were pain
stakingly done wrong
Because years later have we corrected
the harmony
And has our past made us the perfect
melody to our song
See people don't understand there is
growth within the storm
I have been going through so much
now
That I am perfect when it comes to
what not to do
Compared on what to do

Things that have been so
misunderstood
would make a person wanna climb
back in the womb
And try to be reborn
Try to have the water that is suppose
to cleanse you when you get here
Be the water bag the burst when you
are on your way out and have not yet
been scorned
Because in life the abdominal pains
are still constant
Regardless of the passion that a
human vents
To preclude the illusions that we all
have from
Uncertain past situations
We all have been addicted to
something that
Makes you remember certain
accusations
So with that said
I am here

D.N.A.

When you see these letters do not mistake them for a woman who does know who her children's father is

Know that these letters simply mean **DO NOT ANSWER**

For the man who calls you who made promises that he knows that he can not keep. **DO NOT ANSWER**

For the man who calls you in the middle of the night after 11pm. **DO NOT ANSWER**

For the man who calls you because his woman is not available. **DO NOT ANSWER**

For the man who tells you he loves you and he was just with someone else. **DO NOT ANSWER**

For the man who says he is out of town but he is really in town. **DO NOT ANSWER**

For the man who has no car and calls to borrow yours.
   DO NOT ANSWER

For the man who calls you to take a loan out of your 401 k. **DO NOT ANSWER**

For the man who has 10 kids and wants to be the daddy of one of yours. **DO NOT ANSWER**

For the man who calls you from the D.O.C. because he failed to mention a couple of felonies. **DO NOT ANSWER**

Now ladies we can avoid of stressful situation if we just learn to. **DO NOT ANSWER**

Collaboration with my big sis.........
Rhonda Pickett, Chicago Illinois

Chapter

I'm beginning to learn

I am beginning to learn that everyone
that approaches me
Is not for me
I am beginning to understand that
everyone that states they love me
Is not real love at all
I am beginning to live the life of
cautious
By any means necessary
I am beginning to realize that words
that hurt
Are words with truth or words spoken
by insecurity
I am beginning to learn that it is okay
to be alone
I am beginning to practice patience
and live my life in a zone
Zone that consists of breathlessness
and
A peaceful serene of the ultimate NO
No drama, no tears, no arguments, no
questions

Just me
I have learned that love is not bad
Time invested is not waisted
It is what you took from that situation
to make you better to
Be able to help someone else out
I am learning that there are jealous people
But there is a righteous jealousy and it is only for God to use
I am learning to be still
Be still and wait
I am learning to not be the victim all the time
And learning to walk away with pride
I am learning that some will not learn
But I am learning that I have learned
I am learning that I am still learning as well.

A Prayer Given To Me By A Personal Friend By The Name Lester Spoken Sylence...

Father in the name of Jesus, I want to thank you first for the gift of life. Too often God do I look at the trials of this life and forget that you are an incredible God. Today I want to recognize you for the Great Provider that you are. You've been my friend and comforter and I love you with my whole heart. As we pray today, I am speaking to you on behalf of my sister and your daughter. Today she is troubled in spirit and we need you now to speak to the depths of her heart. I do not profess to know all, but I know that you do, and in Jesus' name I ask that you come close to her room now. Silence the voices that would oppress and depress, clarify her immediate surroundings and remove any stumbling block whether it be human or otherwise. I pray now for peace of mind, and I trust you today that you will receive this prayer in the faith that it is offered up. In Jesus name... Amen.

Want who wants you

We all have that special spiritual older person in our lives that has advised us wisely to want who wants you. If there is a man that you want, that does not want you, that relationship is doomed for failure. A man who wants you will stand by you, unconditionally. You will not be dating for 10 + years. A man will ask you within the first 2 years to be his wife if he wants you. He will not mistreat you, he will not misguide you, he will not confuse you, he will not lie to you, you will be his queen and the center of his affection, NO MATTER THE JOB HE HAS, THE FRIENDS THAT HE HANGS OUT WITH, THE GAME ON TELEVISION, he will be genuine and sincere in every movement concerning you.

Now let's deal with that man who doesn't want you. He is the COMPLETE opposite. He is filled with games, confusion, multiple women, (probably a wife); potential STD's that he plans to pass on to you with no regard for your safety, mentally, physically or emotionally. He will play as many games with you as possible. He will never be dedicated to you, he will never make you his wife, he will never give you the respect that you deserve and why because he does not want you. Now if that man says he does, he just may want you for the moment. So do not be confused with that man who does not want you and the man that does want you. The man that does want you is going to go out of his way to show you that he wants you and only you. How do you know this man, he is the man that you constantly look over, he is the man that listens to you when no one else does, he is the man that is in your closest circle of friends. But you say ohhhh he is just my friend.

Take a second look at that friend Girl!!!!!!!!! And want who want you..........

**Collaboration with my big sis.........
Rhonda Pickett, Chicago Illinois**

A Grandma's Heart

I talked to my grandmother this morning
And the sound of her voice made me want to just
Lay up under her love
Over the phone she expressed how she was reading her bible
And how she loved God because he gave her wisdom and always enough

She said many things as she often does
But this time she was so happy to hear from me
As she expressed her sweet melancholy cares from above

As we talked about having gratitude for life
A small tear arose from the corner of my eye

She said I hear concern in the
whispers of your voice
She said baby what wrong, what is
all that noise
I said what u talking Lucy bug; it is
peaceful on my end
She said naw baby there is rumbling
in your spirit and the nasty devil is
trying to win

As I listened to her speak
I was filled many emotions that I tried
to hide
Because even over the phone my
grandma knew me
Even though I tried to fool her with
my carefree lines

She stated remember that God gave me
instinct over mine's
As she spoke in her soft mellow little
voice
I said I am yours and I am fine, she
said oh but your not

you are lying to yourself
She said don't you know you don't
need anybody
For you to come on thru
She said what you want is what is
haunting you
She said I'm your grandma and it's
alright to be confused
She said this world out here that yall
live in
Is filled with fleeing fools
As I laughed she stated see that's all it
took
I've been on this earth 84 years
And I have learned and witnessed
from the good book

She said I had a lot of kids and I
lived my life for them
But I can sit and smile and say
Thank God I made it
And only because of him
As we continued to talk with a smile
on my face

I laughed at how quick she said she
had to go
Of course it was another grandchild
on the other line
That also needed a conversation from
time to time

She said Lyrical my child, you know
how they say never let them see you
cry
And I said yes
She said the desire of your heart starts
with grandma's chest
I said what does that mean
She said I taught you all to love and
be in unity with my heart
She said that is why I knew something
was wrong because my heart and
yours was not in sanction from the
start

She said now you are back on track
and the sound is clear as the wind
that blows

Because you are my all day worry and my midnight dream
And tranquility will come with the more you know
She said pick up the phone more often and Ill keep you in check
But let them see you cry, and my words will take care of the rest.
She stated walk a way with a smile my child, and put on you a pretty dress, I said actually I have one on today she said well good my baby because to the world you're just a woman
But to me your one of grandma's best....

Love and Fear

Sometimes when you are in love, situations can cause hurt that pulls at your heart. You become stuck in a place
where you are not sure which road to take. Do you leave or do you stay. You are stuck in between trying to get out and trying to work things out.
Even when you are in the best relationship, things can go sour. Sometimes it's better to just let go and maybe move on. Pray about everything though, because when you acknowledge that God is in that storm with you, things start to get better. Prayer does change things. Might not change the situation you are in, but it will change you.
Relationships are hard work. What you did do get that person, is how you

remain. You can not switch up like the weather climate.
But when you are in a situation that you keep coming or running back to, you need to look at that. Will it ever change or will games just remain to be played.
The other person is always going to expect you to be there. That is when the damaging of your heart begins. And as silly as that might sound it is true, because the words that you said will come back to haunt you.
We always get signs when something is not right, love does not hurt.....but it is a 9-5.....

Questions

Have you ever known for God to place something in front of you for it to fail you? Have you ever known for God to direct you down a dark path and there is light at the end of the tunnel when you thought there was none? Have your ever cried out his name and he not answer right on time? Have you ever been so distraught at life that you wanted to say fuck it all? Have you ever been so tired that you are just tired of being tired? Have you ever just wanted to just understand why there is a black cloud over your life? Have you ever just wondered are you the problem? Have you ever just reasoned with your self to do better but there are still few results? Have you ever just developed a sense of sorrow? Have your ever really just listened? Have you ever just stepped out on faith? Have you ever just really let it go? Have you ever just let love find you? Have you ever just stopped and thanked him? Have your ever though about if dark nights mean anything? Could they mean that there is a sunny day coming? Have you ever thought that nothing will work with out God in it? Have you ever just wondered why God will not send you the person of your dreams, what is taking so long? Have you ever thought about just working on you? Have you ever just stopped and allowed him to work? Did you ever think that maybe he does not need your help? Have you ever thought things are not working according to him because you are not doing as you are told when you hear him? Does he give you signs? Do you believe in them? Will love ever truly come around? Are these questions making you think?

Scriptures that I love and helped me

For many are called but few are chosen ~ Matthew 22:14

Be still and know that I am God ~ Psalms 46:10

Faith of a mustard seed ~ Matthew 17 20-21

To learn to let go ~ Proverbs 29:11

When you are crying ~ Acts 1: 7-8 and John 14 1-31

What love really is ~ 1 Corinthians 13 4-6

When someone has hurt you ~ Hebrews 13:5

And they will help you ~ Lyrical

As A Woman and As a Man

As a woman you are worth being number one
You are worth that time that made that man work until he was graced by your presence
And as a man you are worth a woman who respects you and that cares
Both should take the time to make sure that is everything is there
Love is what it is, love is what it is
Just because things may or may not have worked
Does not mean that love will never come
As I write of course I am a woman scorned
And have went through an abundance of different things

I am learning to let go and let God
The creator of all human things
And have been placed on that path
To know that there is someone that is for me
It is like a palm tree that withers in the wind
When the tornado is about to hit
It might get half way to the ground, but it always gets back up again
That is what someone who is hurt goes through
Never settle

The person that hurt you, I promise they will call
But this time, on the other end your hurt will not show
Because you have learned to let certain things just go

STOP!!!!!!!!!!!!!!!!!!!Warning signs

You could have avoided the mess that you constantly find your self in, if you paid attention to the warning signs.

Now let's visit some of those warning signs

If a man says that he is MARRIED but getting a divorce and that was 3 years ago........ STOP!!!!!!!!!!!!!!!!!!!Warning signs

If a man is taking his wife on vacation, but he no longer loves her and he will talk to you when he gets back..... STOP!!!!!!!!!!!!!!!!!!!Warning signs

If a man never answers the phone when you are around STOP!!!!!!!!!!!!!!!!!!!Warning signs

If a man never answers your calls, but instant messages you or calls you back, or even texts you.......
STOP!!!!!!!!!!!!!!!!!!!!Warning signs

If a man starts bitchin over shit that is so irrelevant and not worth bitching about........
STOP!!!!!!!!!!!!!!!!!!!!Warning signs

If a man has nothing to bring to your table and everything on your table is good for him........
STOP!!!!!!!!!!!!!!!!!!!!Warning signs

If a man states that you are intimidating because you are on your shit and don't take no shit............
STOP!!!!!!!!!!!!!!!!!!!!Warning signs

If a man allows his baby's mama to continuously call your phone with no intervention..........
STOP!!!!!!!!!!!!!!!!!!!!Warning signs

If a man has been laid off and has no intention of finding gainful employment and thinks that The Department of Unemployment and is sufficient enough to live on........
STOP!!!!!!!!!!!!!!!!!!!!Warning signs

If a man can not respect you for the woman that you are and respect all of you but tries to change you into the woman that is good for him........
STOP!!!!!!!!!!!!!!!!!!!!Warning signs

If a man does not have God in his life and is not trying to learn about him.
STOP!!!!!!!!!!!!!!!!!!!!Warning signs

We all have choices, we just have to pay attention to the warning signs...........

**Collaboration with my big sis.........
Rhonda Pickett, Chicago Illinois**

You (readers)

Right now I got fire in my heart
Right now I need to speak so let me start
See I am in a situation where I don't
Know if I need to stay or need to go
But something is telling me I got to sacrifice
And let this situation finally float
Float away and decenergrate in to memories
Some good and some b ad
Some thought that I should not have
As women we get overwhelmed with angers and whys
But the whys are because of what we accept and allow in our lives
I'm like Jill Scott my heart is raining
And I know you have been there too
I want to be like this song in the background
Just so soft and smooth

But things and situations allow us to be taken
Out of our element
And that is the exact reason why
We be going through
We make people priorities when they tend to make us options
Like we are a game
never the less it is our fault
That we allow bullshit to make us insane
Close your eyes sometimes
When the world just seems to get too much
Sometime you need to allow your mind to
Just get out and go somewhere......

Just Take a Moment

Just take a moment to think about through everything that you are still here
Through out all of the adversity that has come your way
 Through all the times God could have taken you away
You made it and can say I am still here
 Still here when we thought we could not take anymore
Still here when people walked out of our life
 Still here believe that there is life outside that door
 Still her when shit got shut off
 Realizn it was not that bad
Still here when thing that we thought mattered really did not even compare to what we had
Still here when people said we would

be nothing without them
Still here when yes we can be a bitch
or an ass
When we really do not have to act
like that
Still here when people have talked
behind our backs
Still here to say YEP, I even laughed
my way through that
Still here after we have been hurt
and wronged
Still here when they tried to come
back
But our door finally said no return
Still here when I even walked right
into death
Still here because even I have
something left
Still here when the pain has been so
bad
That we prayed for God to allow us
some relief
Still here when others have made our
children options

And still think they have the right to
speak
We are still here when our children
need someone to lean on
 Still here even when at that time we
might not be strong
We are still here with all the mess
that has tried to consume
Our existence
We are still here because if you just
take a simple moment
And relax
Something's are not worth beginning,
and you begin to learn to resist them

Curve Ball

I am in a world of my own
And sometimes I do not express it
Cuz I got a lot going on
You think that people would know
that you love them
Because you say it
But I am one to know that it has to be
shown
See I am not perfect, nor do I try to be
If I was flawless, I promise you would
not want to know me
I would be to arrogant, to pompous, to
full of my self
And too disgusting
But instead I have a heart that does
not lie
I have water that fills my eyes
I have times where I need to be alone
Not because I am selfish
But to keep me away from feelings
being shown

See when I am almost thru the door
A curve ball hits me on the small of
my back
To let me know things will throw you
off track

So now my guard is always up
When I feel the wind from the ball
whipping around the corner
I have my catcher's mitt ready
I catch that bullshit
That curve ball has no owner….

Fanning Myself

I am so emotional lord
And some may get tired of me talking
about you
But I can not stop
I hear certain things and I weep
because you
Have been so good to me
You keep motivating me by your voice
By your signs
You have begun to place people in my
life
That can never be replaced
You have me hearing melodies that
only I can sing
You have me having this look of pain
on my face
Which is really a good face because I
am so mentally focused
No one really knows where I am
No one knows how fast I type to get my
feelings out

No one understand my struggle is now over
I do not know how to thank you enough
So as I write this and the tears begin to flow
I am overwhelmed because now I know
I know that your love is so real
It is like a feeling that I want everyone to feel
It is a beat that goes deeper than base
It is an octave that is higher than the treble in this case
It is a walk that is combined with a talk
Of a maturity, security, warmth, patience, virtue
Deliverance, fullness, resurrection, gratification
Motivation and stimulation of what is unbelievable
No matter what I have been through
I can look back and just say thank

you for bringing me this far
Thank you for allowing me to push
through the door finally
And not stay there because I felt like I
could not get out
I know that you love me because I am
a different individual now
I am better than I have ever been
And those that read, most understand
What it feels like to be on another
plantation
Called cool water with salvation……

I can not write anymore………..not
today….

Thank you for letting me gets my
praise on, through my words.
Fanning myself

Last Night A DJ Saved My Life

I was having one of those days
So I called up my people and said lets ride
I went in my closet and I knew
What ever I put on was going to
Cause some people to commit suicide
As I got my self together
Took a glance in the mirror
Grabbed my keys
Saw my own shadow and even it looked good
I had a cold breeze down my back
That created an a toxic shiver
I knew what my night was about to be
I drive to pick up my fam
And we step into something to do
All eyes on us
Couldn't do nothing but laugh
They were just as put together
No one knew what the other was going through

As the music is playing
And I am getting eyed from across the room
I put my drink down
But low and behold someone else steps in that view
The dj was on point; it was like he was playing everything I needed to hear
And just to think I was planning on staying at home for another night
When I new my body needed to be sterilized
Sterilized with music and eyes from all over the place
My vision and mind needed to be released
From earlier in that day
I needed to be free
The beat kept making my head jerk
He was playing everything for me
The dj did not know he saved my life
From doing the repeat of the other night.......
NOTHING

I Woke Up.

I woke up this morning with a different mind set
I realized that my life was not over yet
I stretches my arms and put a smile on my face
And worshiped him, for giving me another day
I accepted that all things I can not change
I made mention that I was going to be okay
The sun was out as it always was
But this day was different just because
It differed from all the rest because I made it that way
I changed my attitude and decided to do my thang
I opened up my curtains and stretched my arms
I tilted my head back and let the sun hit my chest

With music playing in the
background
Finally the world was not ready for
me
I thought I had already let people try
to run my life
Make decisions for me, when I could
do that on my own
At that moment I decided to reclaim
my life
I decided to take authority to reclaim
mine
My independence alone was enough to
be proud of
My accomplishments that I had made
to some were unheard of
I had been released of all the boulders
that were trapping my heart between
different walls, at that very second
I took authority over my mind,
happiness and peace call
To be free from stress and to let
anxiety pass me by

Taking things one day at a time
Is what I have chosen finally
Up , up and away
Nothing in my way
Released from all that has a grip on
my essence
I am in control now and I am exempt
from
the devil of depression where things
can
Become transparent

For The Men.........Show Me

Show me love sometimes
When others in these streets seem not to care

Show me love sometimes
When your eyes meet me and I am in despair

I need you to know sometimes that you are my air

Be a friend to me
Even when you actually should be a little mean

Forget me then, forget me now
But show me love when it hurts somehow

I need you near, closer than before
You were the one that showed me love

I Am In Love with the Thought of You

Lester Spoken Sylence Howard

It has been said that only one man ever walked on water, but I tell you that I've been walking on water for some time now. My tears have watered my path for so long that I have forgotten what it feels to have the earth beneath my feet.

Lyrical Eyes

Believe me I understand
I don't even really know you
but my mind is telling me that you
possibly could be the one for me
Could I be the earth beneath your
feet?

Do I even want too?
Or do my thoughts just keep me safe
With just thinking of you
see you came through like a thief in
the night
penetrating everything that had been
dry for so long
it crossed my mind that I was in love
with you
but clarity stated that maybe I was
just in love with the thought of you
see the conversations that we had
from the late night talks in my bed
to every call that comes thru my
phone
I want to be you
but again let me slow down and stop
thinking so hard
cuz I am walking on water with my
thoughts with you

<u>Lester Spoken Sylence Howard</u>

This water is not contrary. Although

tears are not viewed as such, mine have been my meat and they have kept me from succumbing to the voices at midnight. Walk with me upon this love that seems as unstable as water itself, yet is as relentless as the sea when they eye of the storm is near. I sense that now...for you moved upon the dry places of my heart...the perfect storm. I've never embraced the hand of destiny, but if this is what it feels like, then again...I bid thee...walk on this narrow path of my tears with me.

Lyrical Eyes

Tears that have carried me
throughout my years
that have been my comfort
that I can say at least they have never failed me
they show me love when I am not my self
I am unstable but I need stability

Damn could this be you, no gotta just
keep making it be these thoughts
This meat that you talk about
I have used for dinner to pacify
myself
I seasoned it with just enough for
Me not to share
And not to care about anyone else
But I don't want to be like that
My thoughts are so unclear right now
because of the whys and what ifs
see I have been down this road of
uncertainty
and the thought of you keeps my
mind performing for me
it is a resurrection of that perfect
storm
that does not drip a bit of rain
but the thought of being in love with
you
keeps reality from becoming such
pain

Lester Spoken Sylence Howard

We have so much in common. Can we somehow move beyond the meat of these tears to the substance of what is true? Love was never meant to be contained...it only contains. Let us walk in it, rather than fall in it. Each step we take shall take us to a place where tears are but a distant memory of the reality of yesterday's pain. If this is but a dream, then forever shall I remain in this comatose state, until the breaking of the dawn meets me in this invisible world of you and I...when the sun shall announce our coming.

Lyrical Eyes

announce our coming......
darling I hear you loud and clear
see maybe I am in love with the idea
of you

and I have to be honest
and maybe that is not you
you make me warm where my heart
needs to be cold
you make love to my essence without
even being near
my mind wanders to that white picket
fence
even to my wedding day
seeing your face and knowing that I
did right this time
I stepped out and I gave my thoughts a
try
and my thoughts saw me through
and actually this time I was seriously
in love with you
see I catch myself wanting to be that
rock for you
because every man needs to lean
and that storm that you spoke of
was worth everything in between
I'm a woman and I am scared
and just have been disappointed
time and time before

and my thoughts at least wont hurt me
so that is what has me hesitant to knock on your
patiently waiting door.
But I want to trust you
and something is telling me that I should
I need you to come out of that comatose state
and realize that men before you have caused great pain
but I guess you were right.... That was my life yesterday

Lester Spoken Sylence Howard

And if we live in but yesterday alone, we are all men most miserable. And if we long for tomorrow alone then we shall lose the essence of what today holds. The thought of being in love with me may be all that I need to be for you. Anything more could very well break the sacred bond that we now share. My dearest love...I'd rather spend an eternity in your thoughts than to risk the eternal pain of trying to grasp the wind

Bringing something to the table

On my half of the table, there is employment, on my half of the table there is a vehicle, on my half of the table there is plans for retirement, on my half of the table there are plans to secure the future of my children, on my half of the table there are goals, on my half of the table there are things that I need to not only maintain a comfortable life but a life that is conducive to my well being. On my half of the table there is love and compassion, faithfulness, honesty and support.

With a table set this way, it is fit for any king that is worthy. What are you bringing to my table?

Collaboration with my big sis.........
Rhonda Pickett, Chicago Illinois

You Are Worth More

How many more agonizing nights
Do I have to continue to try to make
since of this madness?
when I know there is nothing left
except sadness
being able to look at others be happy
Those have not had to work as hard
as I did
maybe that is it; I had to work for
happiness
and that simply was not the regimen
for our success
I dealt with so many things that point
blank are embarrassing
but shame on me once or twice but
the third time
change needs to come
I transformed into this bionic human
that realistically could not keep up

with your mess
no matter how much I loved you,
you downed me and degraded me
when
you were the one that was insecure
and
did not know where you were going
I became imperfect in your eyes even
though
I knew I had flaws and was not perfect
however how you began to treat me
after
all of the years and time that was
invested
left a permanent scar
that still to this day bothers me
I cannot lie.
I should have known all along that I
was worth more
when I got you out of my system
people and things were so much more
easier to deal with
but because of you, I carry around
uncertainty

which at this point in my life I am
working on
I cannot believe the strong dislike that
I have for
some one that I actually was so in love
with
but that is just how life works and I
am happy to know that I am not the
only one
I feel sorry for where you are now
but I am worth more than even caring
about you
so at this point you no longer exist

Words When I Was Going Through

Let me be your inspiration
It is going to be okay
God is just using you right now
Just hold on to his garment and pray
Drop your tears when things get you tired and weary
Scream if you have too and then rest easy

The Resurrection of the Heart

There is a young lady
Whose heart is sour
She has been tormented by a man's power
Not knowing that she holds the key
Because he is not worth anything without she
There are other men that are men and not he
She controls the motions
Though she feels like she is motionless
She has not developed her essence
Though her emotions have been caressed
She eventually will realize her hurt
When she feel like there is nothing left
She cries at night not knowing that she is getting stronger

That God is using her at that very hour
Her soul is being touched
She is being blessed with so much
She will be able to soon stand
And this sister will not need this man............

One of My Breakthroughs

Sometimes I think of what I should write
Then all of a sudden these words come to my sight
I let my pen guide me through each and ever line I touch
Then my heart gets to pumping because I need to publicize so much
I realized I could write when things would just flow
And my feelings and emotions would come through
And that is all I would know
I use my visions of life and experiences to speak to my heart
And I put it on paper and it is a match to a spark
I try to express all that I can, not verbally but pen to pad
One day people will need to understand who I really am
They will read what I write and feel

my emotions through my hands
Some say I'm unique
And I say I am not
I am just living my talent through
Gods divine plan

~Lyrical Intellectuality~
[Lyrical Intellect Part III]

Lyrical Eyes

Part 2 said for writers only
and Part 3 says for writers only as well
because we live in a world of worldly attributes
when what we need are analogies of custom fitted poets that are in solitude
many do not understand that we are the most loving people
that do not entertain drama
but we are placed in situations that cause nasty aroma's of anger.
Anger that make one not understand how easy it is to verbalize how we feel on level that are not in between, but that are in countless sheets of paper with marks of black and blue words that have caused one to write how

they feel down
to make transparent for one to hear as only
if we were their parents to make them
understand what is dear to us.
I soak up words that make me code
I sometimes have to look to the sky for
an E.K.G. monitor to start over again
so that I can be back in mode...
to sympathize with others
because I have been where no one
wants to go
I am now able to love everything that
comes through my path
and tell them the simple words of I
love you—
to make them understand where I am
going.
Lyrical shows herself new every time
that she is allowed too
She takes nothing for granted
not even Part 2 that she read
that created her silence to come back
from the dead

to allow one to see that she was still here
and that this was her year to Thank the most high
that I love and for him I would die
while tears of gratefulness would flow
for thanking him for picking me
as one of his instruments that can blow
verbally and mentally
spiritually and physically
For my stage is set
I need no applause
for me to walk off stage
see I am coming back
to challenge any dialogue..........

L. Lorelle Dottery

I have no problem with expressing my great excitement
and enthusiasm for possessing a high level of intelligence...

In Jesus name, I speak to the
mountains that seem to be
high enough for me to not have the
proper equipment... Nevertheless.
With that mustard seed faith of mine,
God can turn that once high
Mountain to a beautiful low valley...
day dreaming about living
In the shade of such a place, adoring
the love of your words and the
Fact that I can just fall for one word
that you say within that shade
And get hot all over again..
The world will never understand, so
instead of banning this world
of the blind, I take the Writers Only
sign down, schooling those:
Hungry for words that don't bother
coming out... Because of no faith...
One of many reasons of why he's so
double minded and unstable in all
of his ways...
Speaking my words in your presence...
In this heat, blowing word for word

on your soft skin, cooling down a
piece in need of staying soft... Sweet...
Luke Warm.
Adoring, a sight for sore eyes, because
I'm no longer in the mood for
Starring, and picturing something so
beautiful step down from its position
to become so frozen... So torn...
Life being so short, your
intellectuality not even capable of
being seen by
that particular sight...
In this short sight, all I spy is anger...
And Anger causing the precious to
fall,
at the same time singing
harmonically "We Get Up",
strengthening the life
Span no one thought could be
revived...
Conversations with my Lyrical
conscience starring in her Lyrical
Eyes,
Picturing a wonderful story unfold...

It's like the longer I stare in her eyes, this story comes in second from the Greatest Story ever told...
Staring for so long without blinking, tears beginning to flow everlasting Liquid from my eyes... Having an epiphany on when looking up, I spy God giving me the Fountain Of Youth, which explains this water in my eyes, and of course
It's marvelous in mine eyes, so I keep crying only to find myself wrapped under
This... Lyrical wing, flapping freely: to a world far beyond this one into a kingdom
Outlined with a Golden light, with doves helping out to open this pearly gate...
Reaching that gate, only to hear a woman's
Voice constantly saying: "Lorelle, wake up!".... [I was never sleep]
Back to the stage I go, in the footsteps

Of My Lyrical Conscience adoring those
Things wonderful in the sight of a naked eye
as she continues to show...

Lyrical Eyes

As I walk out on the stage
sweat pours from my head
because no one human can understand
all the words that come through my pores
they are like words with a million metaphors
to explain that I am Gods child
no if and's buts about it
I walk to a beat of a percussion
with chimes in the back ground
with a fountain of not water
but the blood of Jesus
covering my mind ,body and soul
taking care of anything negative that

comes in my vision
my words are my armor that protect me
that simply shut people up
make people remorseful
for showing pain and not love
I am here to be a teacher
because my life allowed me to graduate
from the class of being the student
that did not speak
because I consistently had to meditate
of what I would say
As I breathe and release my spine
from being stiff
L. Lorelle's words come in to help me know that beauty
is me which has created my essence to lift
and the gravity that is holding me
allows me to walk off stage
and leave my crowd speechless
with the Writers Sign dragging
and all you hear is............

L. Lorelle Dottery

The Definition of Silence, in sight slowly reaching for my Shirt to turn me around and place an even more Look of Stillness towards our crowd.

Collaboration with Mr. L. Lorelle Dottery from Detroit, Michigan

U Don't Need Anyone

Heart beating, palms sweating, hormones racing
U don't need anyone
Lies told, deception played, games with scores
U don't need anyone
Time stolen, life threatened, soul aching
U don't need anyone
Words stated, days disrupted, silence becomes your friend
U don't need anyone
To make you feel this way...............

As I Lay.................. On The Beach in 06 in the Bahamas

As I lay here on this beach
and feel the breeze hit my face
I appreciate God in bringing me to his domain
Here I am in a place that at home
one would not value
that's why a vacation is sometimes hard to do
Hard t o do because before the vacation
you have to work up to it
whether it be money or time its not
easy to d o, however you have to
As I lay on white sand with my favorite color water
TURQUOISE
rushing on my feet

Tears began to fall
because I miss what got me here
my family, kids, and everything
They got me here through work, sweat
and tears
This is my personal private vacation
and it was well worth the wait

and I came alone with no significant
other
This experience made me a better
person
to show me my worth and let me rest
within my self
As I lay..........
Peace

The Morning Before I Left

Here I am in a world that I always wanted to see
this is an experience that I always wanted to be
I've seen a level of respect that I have never seen
I have witnessed beauty and everything in between
I am at home
I am surrounded by love and these people only know a smidgen of me
You sincerely appreciate things when you are placed in a different atmosphere
but this time God pulled a number on me and showed me I was home since I was placed here
He showed me how a man is too treat a woman
This place is my secret place of rescue
This is my heaven and my paradise
This is where I can come and cry

when my reality is mean and keeps
me held up in time
This is my secret garden; this is my
big bowl of fish
This is my private villa
when I shine as big as the sun
but now I gotta go back to where
things are familiar
Gotta go back to where things are not
always nice or fair
but just gotta remember that there is
truly a place that is better
and believe me I know where.....

A Woman Period

How many times must she tell you
that she can stand her own
Give her a dollar and guarantee she
will turn it in to a home
She don't need you to understand her
past to get you through her present
she don't need you to see her cry, for
her to get to her achievements
How many times must she tell you the
bags under her eyes are worth it
She does not need your sympathy
because God is controlling it
You need to realize a woman is
worthy just like the rest
See in actually stronger because she
gets no rest
see in her eyes she sees further then
right now
see this woman, lets God show her
how
How to believe, how to have faith

How to move forward and simply bow
and give thanks
We are pure, no many how many
times we have been touched
no one can love us more or nearly as
much
he will never forsake you..........
remember he created you
You are a woman PERIOD

It Hurts but Ima Be Okay

I started out this relationship
with honesty
now how the games began
are clueless to me
I put my all in everything that you
and I did
I even went against the grain and
introduced you to my kids
we kept it real with each other
like we were saying for better or for
worse
nothing was hard, nothing seemed as
if it were being rehearsed
I loved being with you
talking to you
imagining things with you
loving you and not thinking twice
about it
even though I knew you were not
perfect
so my mind playing tricks, usually I
could fight it

so tell me how I wound up here
alone like we never met
heart feeling like I made the biggest mistake
knowing that I have no regrets
I let you into my world
I began to have pure feeling of being free
like a little girl
only for you to turn on me and hurt me
to leave and not say anything
to start making decisions that would take priority over us
and quite honestly
that damaged so much trust
we were pure and had no problems
we loved each other so when things that came up
we would solve them
but now you are not here and
and I don't understand what happened
I feel like I am loosing it

but don't wanna tell anybody
because they won't understand
just how much I truly loved you
how to me we could have worked
things out
no matter the involvement
but I can't do it alone
so now my heart sits back in the closet
trying to figure out how I let another
come in and make me feel like
maybe I am not worthy of love
but then it comes back to me
I have to guard my heart
because only I can control it.....

He called to say I love you....

Melancholy Laughter

You are my motivation
For that smile that you put on my face child
You are that raspy laughter
That comes from my stomach to my mouth
Even when you make me mad
You do or say something that makes me laugh
I understand my laugh
I love my laugh
Because it sometimes soothes me
From going back to my past
Past of insecurities
Past of distant memories
That hurt and created tears
Tears that created anger
Anger that created fears
But I met new things
And were introduced to new people
People that were not selfish

But people that were selfless
You see my laugh is not a sarcastic one
It is a comfortable sound
From where I am in my life
It is the music that I hear and that I sing
It is the poetry that I write
That people keep requesting
I realized that a hug with a smile
Sometimes is enough for me

The melancholy laughter
Is a peaceful being
Where one is tormented
Another can bring a person thru it
Harmony, is that of love an laughter
That unity of the morning after
I laugh because I had to learn how to
I laugh because I had to learn simply how to
I laugh because I had to cry but simply learn how to........laugh

Men Have Brought the Bitch Out In Me

Woke up with a different agenda in mind
bobbin my head to some of Drakes rhymes
If you got an Itouch download The Winner
cuz that song is not just for niggas
Its for me at this time
Jazzy new cut in my hair
Matchin underwear
For ones that want to choose to use their minds
A different perspective with mellow lines
Different attitude like fuck it if you want to bounce
Your loss not mines
Your issues did not consume me
I was your security
And my heart was there innocently

You choose to do the fool
And act like I was your tool
So as I cleaned up my house
Listenin to Floetry spit flavor from their mouth
Smiles filled my face
As I lit candles all throughout
I pulled out some 5 inch stilettos
And put on this sexy piece
That only complimented me
I acted as if I was in a movie
And remembered how many options I had
To yes.....do me
The bitch came out of me
And yes met me at the door
Stared back at me in the mirror
blew me a kiss
And the sight even made me quiver
I took my left hand and touched the nape of my neck
Dazed into my own eyes
And said " damn I am the shit..............."

What I am not...

I was birthed from a womb that was
prepared for me too soon
However I am not ahead of my time
I was raised in a wealthy
environment
Contrary to ones belief I am not rich
But indeed I am valuable
My name means Dedicated to God
Honestly I am the first to state that I
Have violated that sometimes
I am not one to be stern or severe
Therefore I can speak with a gentle
reprimand
My eyes are light with color
However I am not sensitive to the light
I am a sensible person
What I am not is heartless
So I am able to feel or perceive
Different circumstances in life
I have these talents of many
What I am not ….is quick to rush

To what I know is prepared and mine
Where I am going is to a location
With no designated time
What I am not is a person that is easy to push away
But what I am is a miracle in transit
I am blessed to be in my own space
What is impossible is attainable
What I am not is inconceivable
One will read up on me one day
What I am not is a southern mockingbird
However my vocals are from down south
I was raised in the northwest region
What I am not is septrional
I am passionate about my self being
What I am not is apologetic for how things come off
I am a very educated woman as many also are
My position in life is that of a strong positive emotion
What I am not is complicated

However what I am is viable
What I am……is simply reliable
The definition of quantity and
quality love…..

A Black Woman

A black woman with a smile
What a beautiful thing
We have perfect breast, round behinds
and also creamy brown skin
We are so sexy and seductive; we can
make a man sing
There are things that tend to make a
grown mans fantasy come true
And make a wise man sin
 We are as pure as a summer's breeze
And as pretty as the water that resides
in the black seas
Our eyes are deep with love
For we are the ones that make life
pleasant
We as women have the4 touch that we
were blessed with from above
We know what we want, and
definitely know how to achieve
We know how to gain success and we

also know how to believe
We have many different features
For believe me we are the rarest creatures
You see we are the most desired and we tend to be that breath that most want to breathe
Our hair comes in many different styles
Short, medium, and long
Our thighs in many different sizes as well
We are high commodity
Are bank accounts swell
We are black women
With much pride and definitely much poise
We are built off of such strong emotions
Our ancestor's song from the valley low
We can be silent and our face can express hella noise
We must know that we are

oppnipotent and intelligent
No matter what type of women we are
We are what carries the torch for a
life to be blossomed into a star
Challenge is our middle name and
our biggest competitor
Are far behind, you must remember
that we charm others life
With our confidence and our smiles
 We are Black Women
With proud tears and straight backs
No matter we are always ready
No one can snatch what we are
How beautiful is it to be something
that no one can change
How calm to the soul to know that I
am a black woman
And every day we continue to
sore..........

I Want You………………….
Is What They Say

What is it that you want?
What is it that you can offer me?
I am a woman that is created from
pure destiny
See the destiny that I am not even
aware of
So yes what created me is fierce with
his gloves
You look at me and you see soft skin
Luscious lips, a round behind
And creativity
But darling I myself was dipped into
The spirit of equality
I am equal to no one
I stand on my own in this world
So sick it makes some hurl
At the thought of this greatness that I
so
Eloquently try my best to perfect

He said he wanted me
Again I ask why
Because the simple answer is
Baby I cant even answer that myself

I see something in you that
is not like all the rest
your grace cups my soul
and makes me feel that love
that I don't want to withhold...

So I want you is what they say
Not knowing that it is his grace
That I wear every day
The softness of my voice
The flow from my words
Never rehearsed
Because I do not have to
Because I will never fail to be me
Me that is loved and that is seen
My name is Lyrical Eyes is what I recite
My level can not be reached I am at

my
Ultimate height
Because I give it all my life works to him
I acknowledge the movement of the essence
Of his angels that cover me within

U say you want me
U say that I am beautiful
But what is it that you want
Or is it just what you see
Because do you know what that statement means to me
Probably not, so let me give you some clarity
U see I am a metaphoric angel
An I am dangerous with my craft
And to me is it more than a beautiful face
Or waxen my ass
You see I come from a land of various Opportunities
it is tat'd on my back

the Cross is what you see
But just don't know what is suitable for me
You can't tell me anything
An just expect the wind to blow
See niggas done made it bad for some you know
But in a nutshell what you see
Is absolutely everything that you think
Yes I am created divinely in all areas
And will still accept wants and needs
My flow is that sweetness mixed with peppers
See before I got that divorce My last name was Mrs. Peppers
And I still carry that memory well
I am a pedestal with abc's
That accompanies me where ever I go
So to want me
comes with much more
My silhouette is even powerful
It makes even my shadow flee
I am not speaking out the side of my neck

Because I am no where close to perfect
But what I am is that woman
And what I am is hard to get......

Letter to God

Hmmmmmmm hey daddy
How are you, fine I hope?
I am coming to you ....wait the devil
is trying to give me a mental block

Let me start over
See daddy I am coming to you just to
say thank you for loving me
When I was in my car this morning I
could not stop thinking and reciting
How much you have given me
You love me like no other
Even the people that you have placed
in my life
I just can't stop understanding and
having questions of why
See you have made me into this
woman
That has experienced many things
that others could not dare to
imagine

And as fragile as I thought I was,
sometimes the knife I keep grabbing
And I realized maybe because you
knew that eventually I would rise up
and be strong
Strong enough to minister to those
That did not think that they could
make it with all of their wrongs
See daddy I am weak sometimes
But I am free with you inside of me
I am free with you inside of me
Some people see the beauty that you
have possessed on my skin
Or the greatness of words that create
metaphors from within
Or maybe they see the experience
without even knowing some of my sins
But I keep going, and meeting those
that have accomplished great
Only to find out that many of them
have the same insecurities
That I see on some days
Daddy you are so worthy and I know
that I am not

But I keep trying to make you proud
So that is why I speak from my heart
I had to grow to understand that
when things are going bad
You are in the storm, see I had to tell
someone this morning
That when you realize that, that is
when your life begins to
make sense
And you can begin to move on
You got me doing things daddy that I
never could imagine that I would do
I am speaking to people and some
don't even acknowledge the greatness
in you
So you know what I do, I remind them
that my father is that of gratitude
And his love is so powerful
And I don't really force them to
believe
But I tend to just keep them close to
me
See daddy I can talk to you, when I
don't feel like being bothered

Or shall I say, yep let me say bothered by the few
That claims that they know you, but still have problems and don't know what to do
Yeah I know that is not right, but you know I would never lead them away from me
I love them to much for them not to see what I see
I don't come to you every day daddy, cuz you got me so busy at times
But you know when I get the feeln you make my visuals come to life
And that is when I am at my best and begin to write
There is so much pain around me, so many unsure days
I even got people coming back to me that hurt me
And you know they hurt me in devilish ways
So of course I can't push them away
Well not like they did me

So instead I just smile, and say no thank you
And please go away
Daddy!!!! I am growing and your word said that I would
In Psalms 56:8 is says that you keep track of all my sorrows
And the next day weather death there is still another tomorrow
See I love you for loving me
I can feel your hug sometimes
And when I need that understanding
I go get peace from my parents you are lending
See they don't even know how close I am to you
Well then again maybe that they do
Because they did name me
And Lyrical Eyes
Means Dedicated to you...
Daddy I am a poppet in this world
And my strings are from up high
That is why when I cry (right now)
Instead of using that string to direct my hands

To wipe my face
You take the string that has my head
And drops the string for me to pray instead

Again

That is why when I cry (right now)
Instead of using that string to direct my hands
To wipe my face
You take the string that has my head
And drops the string for me to pray instead

I get chills when you talk to me
But now I have to go, I'll talk to you later
One of my sisters needs me to help her grow......

Love your baby girl

Lyrical....

Triple Threat

Someone an hour ago told me I was a triple threat
They stated I was a poet, could sing and was attractive
And had talent beyond my belief
He stated you are our missing link
He said you are determined and optimistic
And he said I am going to tell you something
One time, see you are dynamic
And as I sat and listened on the other end of the phone
I decided to break what I am and who I am
On down
See Lyrical being a poet, is not something that I like
Being able to sing, has often made people cry
Being attractive is not something I put on everyday

None of these things were something
that I just decided to do
It is what God decided to use me for
in every way

It is like a finger nail, it just grows
and you can't not control it
It is like blood running through me; I
can not live with out it
It is like every breath that I take, my
soul is saturated with it
So with all that I possess in my life, I
did not ask for it

Yes I am a poet, a singer and to some
am attractive
But I am more blessed because of the
objectives
And I did not run from it.
I tackle it everyday and I perform it
see I can be elegant and hood at the
same time
Not because I am either
but because I have the rhythm and
the rhyme

What I am saying is this, everything
that I do is what I am suppose to
It is like an excersism, words are
unleashed
It is like an orange, juice that is sweet
is what I sing
My beauty was created from him, so
what you see is naturally
Nothing fake, or ordeal;
Everything that is in me is real
I am not trying to do anything; it just
comes out of me
Again I can not control it
So again being a triple threat, don't
sleep on it
Cuz I know it.
better yet more than just a triple
threat seriously
some feel like I am a force to be
reckoned with

Now I know I said that being a poet, is
not something that I like
See for those that are artist, they

already know what I mean
It is an inherited disease that keeps me living
It won't and does not kill me
It completes me
I'm here because people need me
To use and then receive me
So again triple threat, thank him
Because I am his puppet
So use me and help me please thee
What I do, you see I did not have to learn it
I just continue to get soaked up and continue to absorb it
I'm this pill in hind's sight I make things better
I don't need a boost
Cuz my life I am already high on it, no need to be clever
Let me stop cuz I am feeling my self
But I'm use to it
Lyrical eyes is not just about pretty eyes
My talent is possessed

so it moves through me
and puts me under arrest with no movement
See I am not an amateur
Most can not tell me what I am
When I am writing, I have this evil face
Like I am insane
And when I am singing
To some I look like I am in pain
But again when things come out of you
Clearly there is some discomfort
But when the melody and words are out
Those that receive me are there to learn from it...

The Shower (My exit..........

I let the water run for a while
Until it became warm and satisfying
My towel dropped as I stepped in
something I thought to be gratifying
This peaceful serene atmosphere
Right leg first then left

Shall we begin......

As the water graced my hair and then
hit my face
And also the body that God had made
I took my soap and lathered up
My cloth to wash away my restless day
all of a sudden as I stood there
I began to feel weak and incomplete
My soul had been broken down
As it has always been
However
Within my pores
My adrenaline leaked
The soap had became this beautiful
foam

Something that I had never seen
It looked as if it were speaking to me
and it said
I am about to make you clean
But I did not know to what extent
So I ignored what my mind was doing
But what happened next
I had know idea of where my hands
would be moving

Follow me.....

The soap was creating this aroma
That I had never smelled before
It was sweet but refreshing with wind
As I stood there
Behind the shower doors....

Continue to follow me.....

So as I stood there
I heard a voice that said you need to
begin to wash
So my hand that was not my hand
anymore

Turned into this exquisite cloth
As my right hand washed my left arm
I heard you are washing away all
that has hurt you
And all that has caused your heart
great harm
you are being given the armor of
power
now take the cloth to the left
continue to shower
Then as my left arm washed my right
I heard you now have the strength of
the devil
Except all your battles you will win
and we will fight
you will no longer live the life of
being disheveled
So as I stood there, feeling possessed
I heard my child now place this cloth
on your chest
We are now washing away misery
Because what you have been through
is called trauma
and you were brought back to life and

now you are at your best
So as I washed as the tears rolled
down my cheeks
He said lather up your towel
It is time to get to greed
As I did what I was instructed

Follow me......

He led me to my legs
He said your temple is a diamond
But you made it a stone instead
He said scrub in between your surface
from where your blood is shed
I heard
Nothing is to enter you
you don't have time for anything
until you are formally wed

As chills came over me
And the water was hot like fire
Tears continue to pour
as water temperature
Tore into my back

I felt like I was being crucified
But God was my anchor on this track

Stay with me........

So as the foam from the soap ran
down my legs
I began to clean my feet
I then heard
This is not going to be hard
How you walk and where you go
For your destination is now you
coming back to me

As I tried to continue to listen
Instantly now I heard only water
Going down the drain and hitting the
floor
My naked body leaned on the wall
And my mind and heart felt like I
was in withdrawal
I could not take anymore
Something was going on and
I realized what had just happened

And was speechless but still my body
was speaking in tongue
from everything that had been
extracted

Follow me.......

He had changed me from a worldly
woman
And had given me an eternal touch
and a race that I had already won
I was wonderfully and fearfully made
yet again
All of my insecurities
And rigid waters
I was being forced to face
Everything was now in my grasp
A poet had been replaced and
updated with Lyrical Eyes
Was now the design that he allowed
my life to create

Now.........

As my hand trembled as I turned the water off
And I reached out for my towel
When I stepped out of what I had just stepped in
I was cleansed, refreshed and remade
All from a shower of blessings that he gave
As I looked in the mirror
Everything looked different the same to the human eye
But what was looking back at me
was something that one should fear inside
She had this look of production
And another look of love
She had this look of seduction

Follow me.......

She was seduced by whom had produced
and shown her the ultimate love

And in the background, there were little wings
And she gave me a strong stare and then a wink
And as I gave her thumbs up, she whispered so clear
Lyrical you have now been made biblical now go out and do your thing.......

The Shower....

The Redefinition of Me

Somewhere in life
You have been abused
You have been hurt
You have been beaten
You have been mistreated
You have been lied too
You have been tortured
You have been hindered
You have been tired
You have been abandoned
You have been tested
You have been broken
You have been disgusted
But now my tenacity is myself
satisfaction
An you will over come adversity
Let no human ever take your life for
their personal gratification
This is my story
I have loved so hard that I begged for
him to stay

Not thinking at the time him leaving
would help me have some space
I have cried sometimes because how
could someone
hurt me as he did
I have laid on the floor trying to
contemplate this shit
I went through things for years that
just tire me to even think about
Things that I am truly not over
but I got to speak on it because
someone
needs to hear the things that allowed
me to get smart
and how I dug my way out
I miss him but I fight it
when I want to talk to him I control it
when I get weak, I remember how
weak I was
when I think of what he is doing I
pray for his peace
many ask why I still care and I state
because his anger
was now my release

My pain was his play do
that oozed through his fingers
This man prayed on me but it was
wrong type of praying
His insecurities hurt my life
my hear was being tortured
and he was that knife
my daddy kept saying
beautiful I don't understand it
why you stay when clearly this is not
love
or is it the devil just has your mind
and you have just not had enough
That is when I work up form the
night an got on my knees
as I prayed and cried
I realized that I was on assignment
and as a poet
what we go through and spit is called
getting on the mic not the stand
so I can testify through the fire
I asked the Lord to redefine me for me
Let me start over because somewhere
I got lost

And started to worship the world and
not he
I struggled with worldly issues
an took the burden on head first
and not remembering greater is he
that is
within me, something that I did not
have to be rehearsed
as I think of things that took me to
places that consumed a lot of my time
I realize the fault in me
because somewhere I was not
living my life correct or right
a friend told me one day b it is going
to take you to fall on your knees
an scream release me as foam sizzles
from you lips
his grace will fall fresh
as tightness from your chest is now
put to rest
To redefine yourself or to me at least
it seems
That the definition is simple
just be what god created you to be

do not get so caught up in a
relationship
that can hurt you or keeps hurting
you
Be stronger than your tears
and over come your fears of walking
away
be that calm when all seems wrong
an know that joy cometh in the midst
of the storm
The redefinition of me is defined to
my heart that of a woman that had to
go through
painful things to see that I could
make it through
to be that voice of words to also help
you
I can be your eyes to see, that with
him I can be a witness believe me
God loves you
We make choices in our lives
that he allows us to do
when I got hit and I got a black eye
That was an experience that hurt my
skin

but not my soul
I overcame that lifestyle
and now my life consist of many trials
but not things that confine me
but things that redefine me........

Let me help you through your transition............ (My conversation with God)

The definition of transition is simply this
the act of passing from one state or place to the next.....
Let's start the process

Alright God, I am angry, hurt, confused and lost
I know that you did not make me to go through such exhaust
Here it is I have encountered a painful ordeal
Somehow you had it connected that emotions is what I would feel
This person I am in love with
No matter what they have done
I was built to be strong
And now I am falling

I thought with them I had won
They mean everything to me
And if you could just give me a sign
I promise this time we will act right
And we won't go off of promised time
I know they love me see that is what they said
But I am so hurt and tired of crying in my bed

Sigh........

Maybe this person is not right for me
And it does matter what they did
Maybe I am just naive because
How we were is indetted in my head
But all I am looking for is love
Emotions and affection to go with a good time
But I just seem to keep slipping
And I feel like loose change
Even nickel and dimes

Maybe that is it my situation was just a game

Thought it could be bought by
hindered moments
That seriously caused me so much
pain

I am making excuses and shit
When I know that I am angry and
Just want this person back
But maybe you removed them because
We were both living off track

Sigh.......

See I just don't know
I feel like I am having an aggressive
argument with you Lord
But you could have controlled this
could you have not
I mean you are the one that placed
our meeting at that designated spot

You control everything so, I guess I was
suppose to be hurt
How could you do this to me?
I feel......

God....

Are you done my child, let me say a few things
I know what you are going through
And I heard you when you called my name
But see first you have to remember
I allow you to make a choice
No matter what you choose
I will always come out first
See what is happening is that
What looks good to you
Is not always for you
And what loves you will not hurt you
And what needs you will not leave you
And what leaves you is not for you
But I am hear to wipe away your tears
Even though many times I have tried to prevent them
See I have given you many signs
But you decided to ignore them

Though I know you feel so much pain
And want me to give you what you want
But what will you learn
If you don't suffer for your choice.
You have options my child
And I created you to do all things
But I have not created you to fall by the wayside
When I should be your everything

'You are in your transition stage and that means
The act of passing from one state or place to the next
Maybe you will allow me to choose your soul mate
So he will never become your ex
See my child yes there is a process
But it will give you peace of mind
Nothing will hurt you this bad
And when you find that one
You will remember this conversation we had..........

Chapter

Hello Poetry

I am upset because you had been here
all of this time
You were my stillness when the world
was moving so
Fast around me
You kept me when I needed to be kept
You consoled me when I cried
You held my hand when I was alone
You became all mine
Something no one could ever take
away from me
Thought they tried
I just wanted to say hello and
introduce you to the world
Many do not even know of you
But that is fine because they will
Because I have to parade you around
I want others to feel like I do
See I am not selfish with you
Because I can accept that you can love
Me and love others at the same time

When I go to bed at night
You are right there, holding me
And loving me and helping
Me create new ideas in my mind
I sometimes have felt like I was alone
But just came to realize that I really
was not
I was just nervous to ask you never to
leave me
Or forsake me.
I know you were given to me
And you were made specifically for
me
So I cherish you
And will take care of you for all the
days of my life
I just wanted to be happy
And deep down inside
You were what were making me
happy
And I just could not see it, or grasp it
I treated you so wrong sometimes
I even allowed others to make you
Feel like you were not important

And I have to admit that, I did let you go
But thank you for giving me one more chance
You are my ocean that waves at me all the time
And I apologize for making tears come from you
You are so precious to me
And to beautiful for me to ever leave
Or hurt you again
We are happy together..........I finally realized that
I just wanted to say in the end, nothing else matters but you.
Hello, how are you doing......? Poetry

Bringing something to the table

On my half of the table, there is employment, on my half of the table there is a vehicle, on my half of the table there is plans for retirement, on my half of the table there are plans to secure the future of my children, on my half of the table there are goals, on my half of the table there are things that I need to not only maintain a comfortable life but a life that is conducive to my well being. On my half of the table there is love and compassion, faithfulness, honesty and support.

With a table set this way, it is fit for any king that is worthy. What are you bringing to my table?

Collaboration with my big sis………
Rhonda Pickett, Chicago Illinois

Finally

Lyrical Eyes

Like a lily that is red, soft with sight
my heart bleeds for you , my mind pleads for you
I have looked and searched
and one day I just gave up
and when I did, God placed you directly in my path
nothing was hard to do
nothing was made up
nothing was with thought
Everything that dealt with the 2 of us was what was to gain
I am scared to tell you that I adore you
because I am a victim of giving my heart away
but your eyes tell a different story
so I am reluctant to begin to worry
You are my calm when the waves rush in

you are that steel that wont even
attempt to bend
I am in awe with you
you are too perfect to become my man

L. Lorelle Dottery

If there was a such thing as perfect, it would be you... I decided to go for a walk one day and God somehow placed me In the Direction of You... Love is in thee air, I must say its True, Thus the Responsibilities that come with being the man of your Dreams, heart, and soul next to God, I am willing to be used and not mis-used, for if that was the case I would fly away, never looking back.. but that's what I get for thinking too long... Putting down my guards after hearing from you the coast is clear. Waking up to a cold sweat then hearing your voice caress: "It's Okay My Dear"... Inspiration to my ears when you

Inspire me to only Fear God, for he can give and take away a Love that was either meant or not.
Never in this lifetime: Would I have thought to give my heart to another heart so compatible from the beginning and think it would last this far. Never in this lifetime: Would I have thought to allow my blood to change from blue to red, hitting oxygen for you. I never saw you coming, and to fall in love at a fast rate knowing you would catch me... I wouldn't have a love like this any other way.

Lyrical Eyes

Your intelligence woo's me
and it keeps me when I want try
not try at all
Because of the unsure part of love
the not knowing is what kills many
people

and when God put you in my
direction
I was sitting there waiting
not knowing that it was you that
would appear
You are my darling
and I want to be with you through
any fear
I want that old school love
that wont disappear because of a
misunderstanding
I want that touch of security
every morning that rocks my world
and claims me
I long for the unity of friendship and
love
mistreating and misusing you
is not something I know how to do
I only know how to love and be
submissive
and true

L. Lorelle Dottery

Being True and being faithful to something as real as God's most precious gift to love is all I ask... make it as if it were thee only task as we unite into one showing the world what its missing. turning certain important heads to seek professional guidance based off of what we simply have. A love inalienable to a cold heart that knows no such thing except gaining love through war. which is so very little to the elites God placed on this Earth starting From Adam to Me. Born in this sin, the question is do I have to worry about I if I know it's pure flesh thoughts and not my spirit man?
A love like yours on my wish list, waking up to you and only you everyday is like Christmas...
taking up far too much time to wake up out of this lyrical slumber, and

when once arising to the Father, Son, And Holy Spirit, knowing our arguments and fights are senseless, I decide to call God's Number.
Love of my life, through ink on a paper starting out with "Dearest", not worrying about negativity in what you found through me, because if not clearly then using the clearest form, I see God in You. ~I Wouldn't Have It No Other Way~

Lyrical Eyes

I love you

L. Lorelle Dottery

I love u toooooooo

God Because Of You

I am happier than I have ever been
I am about to leave a job that was just
a transition
To get me here
I am about to step out on faith
And claim I will make it even better
next year
You are putting me in positions
That my mouth won't even allow me
to speak
Because people will think I am crazy
Because you just keep blessing me
My cup was not even half full
It was at the bottom and I was about to
give up
But I knew that if you created me
That the cup needed to overflow
And that I did not need anything but
your love
You took me out of many situations
And I stayed still and let you move

Realizing that every time I tried to help
I pushed the winning back and just set myself up to loose
It really is not hard to just have faith and wait on you
But I have been in the wilderness
So I can understand why it might seem you won't come through
But I am at the cross roads now
And I see my journey before my eyes
Anything that did and does not make sense, is not worth my time
I am excited about what you are doing
So I just keep praying and living for every other day
Because of course today because of you
You have shown me another way.......

Loving you is simple

Loving you is simple
You can ease my mind
You can release my thoughts
Your meekness is so kind

Loving you is so simple
I see nothing if you are not here
My balance is off
 I need your support to remain near

I see life with you
Knowing that tomorrow will be
forever and true
Loving you is simple
The definition of me and possibly
you.......

Blushing

With tranquility comes a smile
with a smile comes a sense of calm
with a sense of calm comes warmth
with warmth comes understanding
with understanding comes peace
I met this man who just to me seemed
like a God send
he had ways of how he did things I
never really thought of
he looked like nothing I would have
ever choose
but he was beautiful in the
atmosphere
of how me made me feel
everything that would have mattered
to me early on.... now meant nothing
to me
I only cared about how I would be
treated and
the affection that I could give and
receive

His complete ora appealed to me
he became everything that I needed
and nothing that I thought I wanted
but he completed me
molded me
caressed me
loved me to my surprise
and told me
where someone else had badgered me
me invaded that thought and
obtained me
never to leave me
because God was in he
who was a part of she
and never the less
he sacrificed many things
to be with me
He had me blushing and he still does
though he does not know it
I even waited for turmoil
but there is no show of it
He is my weekly work
and my weekend date
He keeps me blushing

I am like a red rose with a hint of
heaven
and everything that I ever thought I
loved
in the past
I now questioned
because this was easy
and then he told me...............
With God, its suppose to be.....

Thug Passion

Funny how opposites attract
Funny how my body vibes for things you attack
As sick as that sound, I'm not perfect either
I also have imperfections
That has me computerized at times
The design of your skin
With tattoos to match
The swag that comes from the way you wear your pants
To the conversation that penetrates
The things that use to adjatate me
Your flow so funk'tified with careful
Dedication of confidence
You have the classification of precedence
You are that of a perfectionist
You finish what you start
With the thug ness appeal of the gutter

With the dark sidewalks that lead to open grounds
At a basketball park
Arrogance and trials have made you who you are
With no concerns of what one thinks
Unless it deals with how respect is shown
To those that speak
See everyone has this hidden ghetto inside of them
He is my light and I am his street
The elevation of us is sick
He is my paper to my news
And I want nothing with anyone else
As we cruise
This thing called life
That man has become my man.....

You bring out the passion in my essence
From your taps on my v shaped
Whew let me not get trapped in a moment today.....

As Jill says… is it the way that you
love me baby
And I am saying yes it is the way
You have forced respect for what you
have been through
How you realize that in the sky
There is still a place for you
How you work day in and day out to
better yourself
To remove what pain still shows in
your eyes
Me as a woman appreciates your trials
Because it shows that you are a man
from exile
Your passion makes me want to listen
And honor the heart of a lion
Who speaks the truth
Not because you owe anybody
anything
It's just the strength of the thug passion
in you……126

Something Pure

You are my muse
For that smile that you put on my face child
You are that raspy laughter
That comes from my stomach to my mouth
Even when you make me mad
You do or say something that makes me laugh
I understand my laugh
I love my laugh
Because it sometimes soothes me
From going back to my past
To rehash self inflicted
Remedies of what was not needed
That hurt and created symptoms
I was diagnosed with the
Diseases called emotions
Anger that created fears
But I met new things
And were introduced to new people

People that were not selfish
But people that were selfless
You see my laugh is not a sarcastic one
It is a comfortable sound
From where I am in my life
It is the music that I hear and that I sing
It is the poetry that I write
That people keep requesting
I realized that a hug with a smile
Sometimes is enough for me

Jesus My True Testimony

From the arch of my lips when I smile
it is simply you
from the words that I speak
though to some are too deep
it is simply you
from the poetry that I write
to the singing that I do
it is simply you
from every morning that I get up
and I drop my head to whisper
thank you
For what is already min an I have not
received it but will
It is simply you
it is simply you
from all of tears that I have recently
cried
it is simply you
from the thoughts that have crossed
my mind
to continue to strive for more

it is simply you
from the conversations and the prayer
from others
it is simply you
for the man that is coming
and the love he is bringing
it is simply you
for the compassion that I am feeling
though I am alone
it is simply you
for the numbness in my finger tips
but I keep typing
it is simply you
for my bible that I pick up
and pray on before I go to a scripture
it is simply you
for those removed out of my life
it is simply you
for the mirror that saw my broken
silhouette
but now sees a rose
it is simply you
from the past to the present
and how I have grown

it is simply you
from the storm that just thundered
and no rain fell
it is simply you
from the patience that I have learned
to have
it is simply you
from the justification of the woman
that I am
and to people that have never seen my
face in the physical
but feel that there is something that
they see in a simple picture
it is simply you
for the days when I am weak and
discouraged
and I get up anyway
it is simply you
for the people that talked about me
and thought that they were right
and did not know that you were
making me better
it is simply you
for me standing up to the devil

when I knew in my mind he had won
it is simply you
for the experience that hurt my soul
but I can testify now
it is simply you
for the love that I have in my spine
that curves in my vessels
that stretches through my arms
it is simply you
for the vision that is color
that shines thru my eyes
it is simply you
for the times that I dropped to my knees
and the pain in my spirit hurt me so bad
and I was able to just lay there
it is simply you
for the pain that rest in my body
whether it be in my mind or in my heart as well
and I fight my way through it
it is simply you
for the dynamics of my persona

in my life
it is simply you
no matter near or far
rich or poor
it is simply you
no matter my scars
though still visible
it is simply you
Me living and not dying right now
it is simply you
for the strength of my heart to protect
my children though I am a single
parent
it is simply you
for me raising my son to be a man
and they say a woman can not do it
it is simply you
for me guiding my daughter and
protecting her from harm
it is simply you
for the hands I hold to pray with
from the lessons that I have learned
it is simply you
from the lectures that I have given

about you
and not worried about what one has
thought
it is simply you
for that long walk that I have taken
many of days
it is simply you

But for the right now, for the joy in
my soul
for the harmony in my bones
for the peace that is in my piece
for the words that are in my mouth
for the tears that are in my eyes
for the faith that I have no matter my
trials
at the end of the day

JESUS……IT IS SIMPLY YOU

Love Yourself

We are in a world of a lot of hurt and restraint
we are in a city of things that are hard to explain
we are in a culture where everyone is for themselves
we are in a society where if nothing is done, dust sits on the shelves
we are in an environment where what we see on TV we think is real
we are in a world that your kin will fight you, steal and possibly kill
But If I could teach just one including myself
to love and feel at ease
to love and be set free
to love and look at yourself in the mirror
to love how you are made and even that awesome figure
to love the stretch marks from

whatever they were caused
to love as if today was your last
to love no matter how loud life
screams with noise
to understand that you do matter to
me
to understand that when you cry, I
simply can not sleep
to understand that if I could take the
pain away
even when I am weak that I can
to help you understand that every
woman and man
was not created for your life's span
to love and hold you when you feel
like you are weak
to love and write for you to let you
know that you are unique
to be your mind so you can think a
little differently
to be your heart so it could pump
more exquisitely
we are in a world where we are
needed to survive

and not loving yourself mentally will
help you commit
acts of Satan's words to put you in his
domicile
if I could get you to listen to where I
have been in my life
I promise you, it will make you look
at your situation
and think twice
Love yourself no matter if you are a
man or woman
because at the end of the day
you are all that matters.....
I love you with no words

Happiness never felt so good

I smiled more now
I laughed so pure
what I wanted was now mine
and I was not gonna quit
I now understood what it meant to let
go and let God
My song was so beautiful
I realized that what I had with that
man
was just for a moment in time
he needed to fly
and my heart would never die
but my situation would change
he was no good for me no way
I started to age because of pain
and I was tired
I was tired of giving a problem
priority over my life
Let me say that again

I was tired of giving a problem
priority over my life
I started looking at things for face
value
if my hands were the hands that were
wiping my tears away
then what was the purpose
the ruckus that was happening I just
did not need
I had to remember what a friend use
to tell me
"Did you forget who YOU were"
and the more that I heard that in my
ear
I had to let everything go
and try that stimulator
called Happiness
and when I got it, it never felt so good

My Yesterday's

The skin that I am in
allows me to express how I feel
and allows me to know that
everything that I went through
is acknowledge and was real
I had been hurt by a Capricorn
but a Pisces came in right on time
I was made to understand that many
things that I endured
was not because of situations
but was because of the man I was
dealing with
a child that had surpassed even being
a boy
he was too unpredictable
but now everything that was in my
path
I was in control of myself
and now I was feeling so irresistible

I became sexy in my own mind
how I carried myself
was not of a woman who had been hurt
but a woman that had been through
just having a
bad yesterday
I could not control what I had been in love with
but I could make better choices for today and tomorrow
and not look back on what gave me heartache and sorrow
I had a sense of having a new life
there was nothing that anyone could do
my past years and burdens did not consume my nights
now I slept well, my tears were tears of peace
and the baggage that one thought I had
another picked up and helped me unpack......... (giggling)

My First Site of You

My first site of you
What could I say?
I was taken back with nothing to say
The man that I saw had this swag
that I needed
I felt that this man was what would
Complete me
His eyes told a story of where he
wanted to be
His heart played a drum
With a ridiculous beat
His name was anonymous
You could tell in a way
That his heart was from the street
As our encounters continued
His hands to my skin
Made everything that was a worry
Melt from within
His scars told a story of reason
Reason for why he still existed
Existed on an earth that was no

Longer fair
Fair to comparison of the fact that life does hurt
However there are twist and turns
Called a chance
Chance to live again
Chance to feel again
Chance to see what's new
Chance to make his existence
Meet his pure sanity
His conversation of quietness
Made his penetration
Make me remember the likeness of
Why he came in to my success
Of happiness
All that I am is for he that is
In a friendship for me
As he grows through his situation
His accusation of anger
Introduces him to an angel with no danger......

Love..............

Destiny Equality

Love a genuine facet scarce and dramatic
It highlights the static that addresses fanatic
The bible says that love is patient always kind
Never pragmatic truly defined
Taken its time to be able to manifest
Is simply perfect even in humility's right
Never acknowledging wrongs even in current light
Love is not sexually transmitted always respected
Never neglects those that are kept at interest
Love has wings of a dove that fly on angels dreams
Able to pardon but never bargains

Happiness love acknowledges
But just as love feels good it hurts
teeters beyond words

Lyrical Eyes

Love is so soft and pure
it completes the ones that feel that
they can not be completed
It is the smirk that is on your face
when you here your favorite tune
It is the look of life lived in someone
eyes under the beautiful moon
Happiness is that pure satisfaction
and gratification
that keeps on classified
in fulfillment and purified
it is that security that is needed
to allow one to be free
it is that walk to ones destiny
Never selfish but understanding
naw its not sexually transmitted
but it is internally and externally

admitted
into the stillness of resistance
of things that can hurt, will hurt and
that try to hurt
but when real love is there ,nothing
else fails
it prevails and swims with the waves
that lasts for years and countless days
it is that kiss that leaves your eyes
open
because you can not believe
that something so wonderful
is happening to thee
it is that candy that is so sweet
that it satisfy and begins to please
and without it you go through
withdrawal
so you want that love to conquer all

Destiny Equality

And indeed it conquers delivers to its
receivers
There are believers and endless
dreamers

Love teaches us patience sharing its graces
Places everything else in its proper perspectives
Love is that sunshine and blue sky
Children playing in the distance
The greatest elations and celebrations
Life granted in glamorous passions
Its those butterflies you get looking at him
That primitive grin from ear to ear
A warm feeling expounded never grounded
Surrounding you with lullaby's
Holding a newborn in your arms
With her sullen cries of joy
Love is even those rainbows
Gods promise after the thunderstorm
Like being reborn and knowing your redeemed
And every hurt you have seen becomes a mystery
Love is individuality separates and restores

It ensures that we are blanketed from harms
Love is a comforter a protector a maker
were the ones too busy taking never returning our part
Worst part is when love is not nurtured and neglected
Taken for granted and rejected mismanaged and salvaged
Love doesn't judge and we don't get to chose who we love
Love chooses us in a realistic rush sometimes we fail to see
Love is you and love is me the way it should be

Lyrical Eyes

Receivers being you and I
destined to be happy in the life time
not knowing who's the next we will love
or who is the next that will hurt

but as today is today
I love as I he loves the church
See when God made me
he made me and you to speak
ever so freely
with the stench of pain that lingers in
the air
we are a sorority of angels
we have out own sorority
called love through our poetry
see I am not afraid to say I love you
I being a person
Love being a feeling
and you being who you are
because as long as I am breathing
I am that distant star
See I care which means that I have to
love
and what pumps through my blood
is secretions of words
that were given from above
I'm not big on what one does not
believe
you see I am here to help you conceive

That because one does not know about love
how can they agree
It is for you and I to speak fluently
an allow them to perceive
I am thankful for my visions
I am grateful for my soul
I am passionate about my talent
because my love is very well known
See he keeps us in the midst of the storm
and loves us through it when we feel like we are alone
But this piece that was so eloquently written
was for Destiny and Lyrical to express our love......

Collaboration with Ms. Destiny Equality from Miami, Florida

Sexy within myself

He said you are as pretty as an angle
I said thank you
I asked him where he had been
I was waiting on him
This man had the alarm to my panic button
He said I want you to know that you are sexy
No matter what you have been through
You are more aware of your surroundings
And I love every inch of you
I love every thing that you do
He rubbed my back
He kissed my neck
He grabbed my hand
Pulled me to the mirror

And he said look at your self
How pretty you are

He said your eyes are like the
First light I see on a deserted highway
He then walked out the room
And there I was
A poet that was speechless
In deep thought

I was in awe with what I saw
All of my woes had made me into a woman
A sexy woman I might add
I knew who I was
And what I loved
I knew what I demanded
And what I needed subtracted
I had grown
I was sexy within myself

That man

A provider
A lover by his own definition
Someone that cared
And showed an abundance of feelings
 Liked emotions and needed them at the same time
Demanded the respect that was due to be given
Praised God in the same fashion
He was all that I needed
And I was the same for he
Our music played in both of our cars
We became forever
I was proud of him and he was proud of me
 And when things did not work
We fought through the society of that break up shit
We lived in luxury in our minds
 And that is what kept us
That man was sexy by his walk, his talk, his demeanor

His security
 He is my wake up call with his kisses
He is my love Jones with me on the mic
He is the truth to the conversation that gets us both high

So in Love......

Words are not easy to say
Regardless of the state of mind you might be in
But I have a conversation that will give you the right motivation to stimulate ones
Dedication to a verse that states..I love you
I meaning this concern nothing else, no one but me and you
Love meaning the warmth of and the emotions that is long over do
You meaning the existence of another
We have been at this "thing" for a while
I am not really sure if you can understand that is taking place
But I will help you figure it out and it will be worth an eyebrow raise on your mahogany face
You might not realize the sincerity of this situation

But I am about to make love to you,
with absolutely no penetration
I can be sexually explicit with just
the blink of an eye
But our relationship will be better,
because I have decided to wait this
time
I am a woman that has lived through
various types of pain
And to express how I feel, I don't mind
and I have no shame
You can either back up or instantly
get it together
You can invite yourself to enjoy the
trust of my pelvis
With words instead of tantalizing
feelings or
Feel how tight I am like brand new
leather.
I am worth the agonizing impatient
wait
How precious is it for you to love first?
And then be amazed?
I will place you in front of me as

being my armor and my shield
You are the image of my soul
It is funny, that I dream of us getting old
You can only imagine
How intimate we will become
The solution will be to set apart something's and convert each other into one
I touched you and say how things could be
And I love you came out
And I knew at the point I became free
You are my step to every walk
You are my conversation before I start to talk
You are my love before my I am me
You are my heart beat, until I die
Simply stated……… I am in love with you.

What a Woman Needs In Him

I need him like a flower needs the rain
I need him to ease away uncertain pain
I need him to control my wave
I need him to walk the road God made
I need him to direct my path
I need him to make me laugh
I need him to fall in love with me
I need him to show me how to love
I need him to make promises
that he can keep
I need him to complete me
I need him to teach me things
so I can learn
how to be
I need him to be proud of what is on his arm
I need him to always posses that charm

I need him to see my dreams
I need him to always believe with me
I need him to go with me to church
I need him to never be afraid to worship
I need him not to stray away
I need him to never lie to my face
I need him to be honest with what he does
I need him to realize his love
I need him to wipe my tears away
I need him to keep the stress away
I need him to be the soles to my shoes
So when I cant walk he will be my support
I need him to walk tall and never short
I need him to be my treble to my base
I need him to be my music in my cd case
I need him to be my rest for when I am tired
I need him to be my fullness when I am empty

I need him to be my paper to my pin
My ink to my subscription
My desire to my dreams
My leaf to my willow tree
My skin to my bones
My all to my alone
I need him to be my ring on my hand
I need him to be my world when we are apart
So our minds are not worlds apart

hmmmmmmm

I need him to be my color to my paint
I need him to be my editor for my words
My journalist to my story
I need him to hold me when I am down
I need him to allow me to do the same
And not think I am disrespecting him as a man
I need him to also respect my plan
and know that he who seeks finds a good thing

I need his mental to be relaxed and pure
I need him to always strive for more
I need him to except that I am a woman first
I need him to expect for me to quench his thirst
I need him to make me special when I think I am not
I need him not to think this all is a lot
I need to not feel shallow
when I fail
or to feel stupid because I am speechless
because I need him to be my scarf
so the cold won't hit my chest
I need him to be understanding
I need him to be outstanding
I need him to be apart of you God
so that we can be everlasting............

Beautiful

I have never seen something as beautiful
It is like crystal turquoise water
With pure white sand
No diamond can compare
Not even a baby's first cry
Waves rushing on my feet with bubbles as if I open up
A bottle of champagne
As beautiful as it is, it has captivated my soul
There was no sound, just a whisper of single waves
It was if I was in paradise with my favorite color.
I really never knew why certain things
Tugged at my heart
But then again I think it was God trying to give me my own paradise
Beautiful and I finally met

God welcomed my heart and that's when my tears began to start
I never felt him like I did that day
I saw what most will never see
I saw my paradise that was strictly for me
And that paradise was my peace of mind that gave me my serenity........

You and Me 20 Years Later............

God is so awesome.............Awesome like a summer's breeze
Like a late night special.........After the day has been complete
20 years of loving you...........20 years of loving you
It's our secret hide away.......That soothes and conquers me
You have been my back bone....When my spine has tilted towards the floor
You created a destiny............That has fulfilled me and has me yearning for 20 more
It has left a permanent imprint of what simply just needs to be
3 kings later that we birthed from boy's to men
This darling was a permanent set up
And God clearly set us up to win.
We have walked this earth as lovers and as friends

My soul is made up of a shield, called husband
A foundation called wife
That is why the pattern that was created from God
You were my design for life.
Every stitch, every flaw— we are chemically inclined
It is not by coincidence that I can not resist you.
Our love has not face, our love has no time
It is something that evolves and stirs my spirit up inside
You are a consistent conversation that moves my heart
And keeps me meditated when I am alone
You control the blood that flows through the vessels, and pumps life throughout our home.
I think to my self………. ………Some can't make it out of the church

Some only make it to 2 years......Some happen to value love
And some make it to do what they once did ....again
In 20 years.
I mentioned God was awesome........I mean so awesome that some might not comprehend
But for those that understand it is so simple
We never allowed the devil to control a situation that was realistically never his
I see you mentally in my peripheral vision for the rest of my life
For the rest of my life................As sure as I capitalize the R and I cross my T
It is not a mistake that you were given to me
I knew 20 years ago, we would still be husband and wife
You see back then and still now........I claimed what was mine.
I love you is a mere understatement of how I truly feel

God placed his hands on us and whispered ....
Simply pray and remain still

He kept us.........................And you are here to witness how it feels to be kept
And when something is created by God
It is always good, and most of all it is always
Real.............

I Love Me

I love me more because of the many
things that I have endured
Many things that have hurt me
But many things that made me
understood
I realized that in life, nothing is
promised
Even though we hear that all the time
But I witnessed it over and over again
All throughout my life
I simply just love me for everything
that I am
And everything that I am not
Every one that I have loved
And everything that I still got
My life has never made since
And I am more alright with that at
this time
If everyday I knew what I was facing
I would give up and force my self to
cry

I am stronger because I was weak
And I am harder because I was not strong
I was naïve when I should have listened
Now nothing gets past me when I know shit is simply wrong
I am here for a reason
No matter what that reason may be
But no matter what at the end of the day
No matter the problem, no matter who has left, no matter the situation
I am always going to love me...

Lost For 5 Minutes

As you hold me
the touch of your tongue
on my back
makes my heart collapse
As I am trying to maintain my flesh
from being weak
you pull my body
and I am saying
please release me from your grasp
but instead you cup my ass
and place your hands on the small of
my back
as the beat of your drums
enter my soul
as you hold me ever so close
I fall into your skin
your scent pulls me in
the tingling sensation runs down my
spine
feeling like cold water
soaking up in reverse from a fire
hydrant

as your teeth bite into my flesh
a sigh of pain and pleasure fill the
empty air
with desire my eyes open
as you look at me
and say release and
let it all go
I whisper
let what go
you say any uncertainty you feel
about you
beauty is you
your past is a distant memory
your present will be your own mystery

I am lost in you.............

I am

I am who I am because of how God
created me to be
If I lived in this world perfect nothing
would affect me
However worldly people do
I will not apologize because my world
that I was brought up in
was much different from you
When God designed me
He created special circumstances and
situations
That only those that were blessed with
me
would go through
We live in a world that if you tell
others of certain things they place
judgment
and call it an opinion
an opinions is just like having a
religion
you choose what you think and what
you do from it

now many may not understand but judgment
is when you judge and think things to be true
only because of how you see it
once again I am different from you

I love different
I speak different
I react different
I accept different
I have been through different
Because of these things ...I am different

Things that have hindered me before
Have allowed me to be a metaphor to a sentence
that allows me to continue to go forth

I listen and learn
I am that woman that simplifies the definition of again
again I deal with internal situations and feelings

that externally you cannot feel
I fluently spit fire from my vocals
because in my life only
because of what I know to be real
Do not fault me for not knowing what
I do not know
that would allow me to be ignorant
and not allow me to grow
A person who can't look at themselves
it is easy for them to speak
and though constructive criticism is
understood
when will you become meek
Frustration and misunderstandings
come from not knowing
but many do not understand because
of what they have not seen

I am who I am
and will stand before I fall
I have fallen before
but remember words are my all

If I do not protect who I am
and my character is invaded
regardless of what you think
My life will remain elated
I will consistently be motivated
Situated
Stimulated
Educated
Sophisticated
Opinionated
Hated
Congratulated
and most of all related to
Who I am
I am me, not you
Or who you are use too.
I have been told many times that my word sting and burn
Talk to my creator he gave me words to express and learn
My desire to be me is even more of an urge
Because I am I am I am

Simply
I am.........

Love Greater Than Relations

I Am Poetry.....

With Love I speak Biblically,
With Love I speak in "Matthews"...
Rejoicing the culture of "The Vital Truth of Love"...
God is the source to love, but seeing that many of us have difficulty loving ourselves,
much less loving God and others.
How can we give and receive love of this high platoon?

Lyrical Eyes

with love I speak mentally
to every inch of your soul
that completes me that keeps me
coming back for more
thanking God for allowing happiness
to come my way

finally.
And I say finally with a sigh
of appreciation for the gratification of
you
for being that man that came right on
time
to save me
I speak to you from psalms
and walk through sand that only God
created
to get to what continues to fascinate
me with us
us meaning you, me and Jesus....

I Am Poetry.....

How great is the love that our
father has bestowed upon us,
that we should be called
children of God!
It was the strength of knowing,
the patient of our moral

excellence that brought us
together...

Living in a Holy
Matrimony...

But we're in that state, because we grasp
the whole concept... We were never angered
by the mistakes that was made in
our transformation...
We was not easily broken,
but easily compatible
because our value of
Love's Commandment
were the same.
Love Our God, and
Love our Neighbor.

We fought & realize that
we love encompasses more
than just emotional affection,

and that it was evidently written
in Journal of FIRST Corinthians....

Lyrical Eyes

No one will ever know the heart that
went into every fight
No one will ever know of the
affliction
No one will ever know the abundance
of strength that it requires for us to
just make it
and to say that we made it
because as we love ourselves we love
One another.
you keep me moving baby in ways
that I can only thank God about
He sent u at the right time
An there is nothing more sexy an
humbling then a man that knows god
A man that lives for me an protects
his home
you are my smile that Adam had

.

when he first saw Eve.
You are my Epiphany....

Collaboration with I Am Poetry from Detroit, Michigan

The Greatest Love of All

My 23rd psalms

My God is my ALL
My God is my strength and my provider, I will never want for anything
He allows me to live, breathe and make choices in my life, he allow me to see all things
That he has made and enjoy them!
He has taken me to beautiful seas and states "Peace be still my child, see the power I posses and know that I am God"
He picks me up when I am weak and my mind is stating that I cannot make it, he allows me to see that my soul belongs to him, and that I can do all things through
Him who strengthens me

He takes to a path to worship, whether it is be the floor, my car, in the shower; I praise him anywhere and at anytime and will all days of my life
Though I have seen things that have tried to kill me, been through situations where I have been wronged and knocked down and even when death has passed me by
But still starred me in my face
I still fear no one or nothing but him, because he created a vessel that pumps for him and he is with me and will forever be
His power and anointing will be my comfort
He is my rock when my table is filled with unruly things that my enemies have tried to knock me down with stress, worries and things that are simply not in my control
Many wake up with oily skin from the night, I wake up with oily skin as well, but that is the oil, that comes

through me in the night, that lets me know that God has anointed me in my sleep and that he is not done with me yet

My blessings and worship I can not get enough of. Sometimes I have to cry because I can not get enough of what he is doing. In the mighty name of Jesus. Thank you

I am blessed and filled from the day I was conceived to the end of the days. I will walk with the worth that I am, because I was created from the most high. I will serve as he uses me and he will abundantly dwell in my heart in my mind and in my soul in his house forever, Amen....Amen

For the new woman that I became thru this process

Flawless In Him

My motive for life is motivation
I was brought into this world to create words
That stimulates my mind that keeps me coming back for more
Because of my dedication
He is my peace beyond the storm because of his salvation
That keeps blessing me to be a blessing to others
To create a sanction
Of stimulation for each and everyone's mind
That is graced with his words that flow through me.
Nothing that I do is for me
I am an instrument in his massive rolodex
And when you look up Lyrical Eyes
You see greatness that allows me to keep going

And singing and spitting for him
I try and touch every man and woman
Boy or girl, and anything with breath
To show him that I have not forgotten why I am here
And that everything that I do is for the dedication and purpose
Of his grace in my eternity.
My pen bleeds secretions of ink
For every reader to think and honor
What they and I have been through?
I go hard because I have to and do not know any other way to be
Sometimes his anger resorts in me
My humanly name means dedicated to God
And my soulful name means that through my dedication
Lyrical eyes was created.
I stepped out on faith to do his richness of massaging souls
Because money can make you rich
But struggle will make you stronger

I have not forgotten my pain that has gotten me through
Many days of inevitable strength
My sores and wounds have led me to crawl
To realize that everything that I have been through
He was in the storm with me
I had to realize it and acknowledge it
And when I did
It is so simple
I became flawless in him.....

Welcome to my world I give honor to him for allowing me to finally share it...... This is what I am here to teach.

~Lyrical Eyes 2010

"It's not the load that breaks you down; it is the way you carry it."

~ Lena Horne

Dedications

Lord, how do I even begin to thank you for this? You designed this before I was even created and you gave me this gift that lingered around my existence. You provided greatness in me and I grabbed it and took off. I love you with every particle that I am consisted of. I will do your will, I will reach everyone that you intend for me to reach, I will give you praise even when I am weak. I will call out your name when my lips are still. You delivered me from pain that most can't even imagine. Though I still go through many things, you continue to tell me to keep going and as I do, you keep me kept. You are my savior, my provider, my comforter, my friend, my everything. I am only a seed in your mass garden. I love you and I thank you.

Everyday I breathe for you, everything mommy has been through and is going through is for what I will not allow you to go through. Learn from me and allow me to grow with you. Lean not on your own understanding as you grow, but lean on God for all understanding. Ashlee, you are a queen of everything that you hold, Camari, you are a king and I will continue to raise you like one. Words can never express how much you are loved by me and how grateful I am that God blessed me with you.

To my parents, there are no words, I love you all. You all are my beginning and my end. My core existence. I am nothing without you. Daddy and mommy for EVERYTHING that you have sacrificed for me, this is for you, I pray you are proud. To my birth mother; thank you for never giving up on me and finding me. You are the reason I am here. Thank you for loving me like we never departed

To my Lucy bug (grandma) Girl you are my energy and my laughter...(yes books make money and I am going to get you your car!!!! ☺)

For my brother's~ Tim, Chris, Jeremy, Shaun and Joshua, your sister loves you like no other woman ever will.

Tim as this was being written you were by my side and I could feel you. I thank God for your life and making you my guardian angel. Though I miss you like nothing else in this world, I know you are fine...Rest in paradise baby.

To my sisters- Lenaissa, Kea, Kelly, Lynn, Cherese, Linda, Laquiesha, Rhonda, Kendra, Banita, Kim, Tirona, Kristall, Bobra, Tiffany, Be Be and Cierra.
For the times that you listened and we either cried, laughed, prayed or we just did us, you are forever in my heart. This is for you

To my aunt Shirley and grandfather that I love so dearly, you watch over me everyday and I can never forget the times that we shared. Tears swell up in my eyes, keep watching over this family. I did it!!!

For my management team…..The Beautiful Ones at Vision2Soul

Michelle Ross
Leah Peters Jones
Sophia Chambers

Thanks for believing in me, we are on our way. I love you for the laughs, tears, prayers and honesty. I'm glad yall are mine!!!!

For the rest of my family……there are no words for the love I have for you. I'm just glad we are family. I'm taking us out of where we have been and to where we always hoped to be.

For my praying mama!!! Mrs. Gloria Randolph, I am nothing without you, you have helped me through my darkest hours and anointed me with oil each time. If there was something more than and I love you, you would have it. You are my everything and I am going to make you proud. God placed you in my life for a reason and I am in yours for a reason. So many hugs and kisses are coming your way from me. I love you mama...

For all of my babies that call me mama…………..Ashley, Sommer, Alexis, Charnelle, Candice, Jaylen, Maya, Jasmine, Jalisa, Dani, Buckee, Mark, Mike, Eli, Miguel, Brenton, follow your dreams no matter what looks impossible. Remember it LOOK'S impossible; but it actually attainable. It is never too late to do what you love. And I will go all the way with you, yall know that. If it is one person that believes in you, you know I do.

For my nephews and nieces whom I adore and there are many of you all, this is for you.

To the best photographer in the world!!! Marvelous Photographs... Marv thanks for putting up with my mess and my crazy ideas...... you know I love you.

To Mr. Kenlo Key......you made my vision come to a form that I will never be able to thank you enough for. For all the talks and the listening. You are a beast with the art work, keep doing your thang, see you for the next cover.....I owe you, you became a great friend.

For Victory Apostolic (Matteson Il) Ms. Tanya Webb, Jaya, Ms.Deana Brown, Rosetta, Ebony, Nina, Kacendra, Tomika ,Tashon, Gretchen, Marques (Killa),Paul Hall, Ms. Philli, Hg Soul, Matt, Percilla........for the talks and the support......nothing but love from me. I thank you.

For the Men that graced my life, to help me with my journey

For my twin with the pretty eyes, who took me by the hand in my teenage years to be the first to battle me in this game of poetry. I have to say this all started with you. You loved me and I knew it and we grew. Apart but still connected in this life of words. This book is for you. I love you.

For my first crush and summer fling when I was growing up, love will never describe us but our experience did. I will always love you Gerald.

For my first real relationship that made me into a mother, I thank you for my daughter.

For my first marriage, I thank you for allowing me to understand a wife's role now and for still calling me beautiful to this day. We grew from husband and wife and became that of life long friends. Thanks for the experience. Love you Pep

For my conviction of 9 years, the best thing that you ever did was to leave me, I thank you……..FINALLY, believe me I can never forget you, I have my son.

For my 5:30am wake up call that I never got, thank you for coming back and the friendship that we now have. You gave me a conversation that showed me that you cared and you helped me make one of the biggest decisions of my life. Love you Tony….04/22.

For you J. Cobb for all the pain that we have endured and been thru in this game of life. I am so thankful that our connection has kept us close and will never let us steer away from what love is. We have a story and a testimony. Keep praying and loving and remembering. I will always believe in you. I love you

For the person that called me pooh, thank you for coming into my life, stirring some shit up and for being that sarcasm that pissed me off to get me here… JFK, 150 all day ☺.

For the love and friendship of the person that prayed for me all the way down south whenever I asked, you my love are my southern comfort and my praying savior of a man.

For my friend that always kept it real and will always tell me about my self- 23rd letter .Bobby I LOVE YOU………. HAHA

For the hottest DJ in the CHI …DJ Spank…….thanks for being you, you opened my eyes to another world and an awesome friendship that will never end.
The Wood

For my always there buddy to love me ,who talked and was honest at all times and name started with the same letter as mine…..B, your time is coming.

For my listening partner that is well on his way, that I will hold down and vise versa until we turn to dust. Trell when I tell you to keep doing you, do it. You are a monster at this game of music that we both bleed for. Let nothing stop you. Nothing. You already know my love for you.

Tim Jones in the Building…….enough said my nigga!!!!!

For the best massage therapist in the world………….Kewon, you are loved… so loved , you honestly massaged my soul. Your sweeti loves you.

For KO'S Barbershop that has loved me and always held me down and helped me with the hhhhh part, Doc thank you and Ko the Barber, you taught me to keep going, I tip my hat off to you. You have encouraged me to become the business woman that I am. I am so looking forward to the moves we are about to make together. We got an understanding and love like no other. I appreciate you more than you will ever know. Thanks for the years of friendship and the love for my son and the love for me.

For my Poetry Husband…..Blaq Ice thanks for the love and support and how you feel for me on a consistent basis. Your Poetry wife loves and adores you!!!!

For the person that I hurt so that they could move on, I am sorry, you will always have that special place.

For the keeping it real men every morning in the cube, words can not express my love for the 3 of you all. We have a life long friendship .Jerome, DaWayne and Walter.

For the person who told me "You are an artist and will always be my baby, you are what Jill Scott is and you have no choice but to be a star.
He stated there is no rush for you to get up because you are only suppose to get up when you want, you are beautiful, gifted and talented" I say to you….we are chemistry with no solution, there are no words for us. I thank God for you. I love you.

For my Kool loc's partner, thanks for being that laughter and check mate, you are becoming everything that I have ever wanted and needed. No matter the obstacles in life, I hope you are going to be here to share it......

For the man that came in like a thief in the night that has understood everything that I have been through and loves me for nothing else and accepts me for everything that I am........this is for you. You are that peace of mind . You are my middle and my end. My beginning was not for you, I now understand that. You are my beat with no verse and I am your verse with no beat. You were the help to get me to my reality. You have become my protector and my friend. You are that phone call away when danger lurks. I honor you, because I understand you. You claim I am a beast but I think that you are. We are in the same art and passion and God has created a masterpiece for us. I just look at it like in this game of life and where we are at, we are monsters together. It's gonna be great and no matter where we end up, friends we will always be......you are my muse......126

We are just beginning ~ Lyrical

For my partners in crime with this game of POETRY!!!!! L. Lorelle, I Am Poetry, Catalina Byrd ,Destiny Equality and Lester Spoken Sylence Howard; become what you are and that is talented angel with a different tune. Continue to serve him and help others through your writings, you all are my love bugs... World look out for them and be blessed as much as I am. You all are

REDICULOUS!!!!!! Thank you for your inserts on this life changing project.

For my local talent that is in the Chicago area. We are saturated and only the great come from our city. We are destined to be heard and you will be as I am now.. Keep singing, staying in the studio at night, spitting whenever you get the chance. You all are my hearts and I am taking you with me. Keep humility in your hearts and be still.

Now for my fans that have held me down since I stated that I was coming out with a book and who stay on me to write, write and do more writing. I do this for the pain that tries to fester but I have learned to let it go and as you read, I hope that you will allow whatever is bothering you to push it to the side and know that nothing is bigger than God. When you know that he is in that storm with you, you know that you will overcome whatever it is.

Be blessed and remain full and over flowing and never half empty. You are too precious for that.

Lyrical Eyes Bio......

And God said.............

There was this beautiful blue, hazel eyed pecan brown child that made her way into this world on October 26, 1976.
She entered in the labor and delivery room, very quietly and then into the nursery. A name was given " Beleshia" meaning dedicated to God.
She began to speak and recite words that left others speechless. It was like she had been touched by God. . Her eyes and what they said were the first. What seeped through her lips mesmerized thoughts and hearts of people. And as years passed her by, she began to hear whispers that stated " write my child write. Use the gifts that I give you, pray on them and I will lead you into life. Say what I put on your mind; let your pen flow like water that

will never stop. You are gifted and belong to me and I have given you the gift of words. Where some will struggle with conversation, I have blessed you with the end result to conclude every conversation. You my child are blessed with a power of lyrics, stay strong my child, it is time for the world to hear it".

I am an African American woman. I am also a mother of 2 beautiful children. That right there says enough. I am very dedicated to my gift that I pose with words. I want you to share in my experience of a different kind of talk. I have been writing for over 23 years and I am only 33 years of age. Imagine that! There is nothing that I love more than being able to express things on paper. Many are called humans; I myself am called a Poet. Many struggle with not being able to have the words sometime but now you have a person that can help you. I decided to write this book of expressions called Relationshhhh VS. Relationships to try and give direction to people with broken lives and broken hearts. I have been in every situation and through prayer and learning how to cope, by me being an instrument for God, I am able to speak his words fluently and I teach through experience. I am a poet that simply gives you the words. Nothing is sugar coated.

God blesses us in many ways and we all have hidden talents, however many do not know what those talents are. You have to listen first and then seek. Don't let anyone stop you.

For additional information and to interact with the author directly, please visit www.lyricaleyes.com

Liberated Publishing Inc
1860 Wilma Rudolph Blvd
Clarksville, TN 37040
info@liberatedpublishing.com
931-378-0500

www.LiberatedPublishing.com

www.ingramcontent.com/pod-product-compliance
Lightning Source LLC
Chambersburg PA
CBHW072002150426
43194CB00008B/967